Foyle's Further Philavery

Chambers

Foyle's Further Philavery

A cornucopia of lexical delights

collected by Christopher Foyle

Chambers

CHAMBERS
An imprint of Chambers Harrap Publishers Ltd
7 Hopetoun Crescent, Edinburgh, EH7 4AY

Chambers Harrap is an Hachette Livre UK company

First published by Chambers Harrap Publishers Ltd 2008

A CIP catalogue record for this book is available from the British Library.

ISBN 978 0550 10436 6

10 9 8 7 6 5 4 3 2 1

Editors: Vicky Aldus, Michael Munro, Elspeth Summers

Prepress Controller: Andrew Butterworth

Publishing Manager: Morven Dooner

www.chambersharrap.co.uk

Designed and typeset by Chambers Harrap Publishers Ltd, Edinburgh
Typeset in Miller
Printed and bound in the UK by Clays Ltd, St Ives, plc

To Catherine,
my long-suffering supporter in all my endeavours

Introduction

For nearly 20 years, I have been collecting all the pleasing, interesting, and uncommon words that I have come across. I might choose a word because I am fascinated by its obscurity, aptness, meaning, or simply its sound. This labour of love evolved into *Foyle's Philavery*, a book that created so much pleasure and excitement that Chambers and I decided to produce a further volume.

Consequently, whilst I had still been expanding my collection of unusual and amusing words since the original *Philavery* went to press, I was clearly not going to find as many words over a one-year period as over a 15-year period, so I set about actively 'looking for' such words from a variety of other sources.

I still take six newspapers a day: five British broadsheets and the *International Herald Tribune*, as well as *The Economist*, *The Spectator* and a number of specialist periodicals. I have 'mined' all of these for their fascinating vocabulary.

In addition to this, the publication of the original *Philavery* stimulated readers to send me all kinds of unsolicited new suggestions for inclusion in a second volume, and I have incorporated many of these. Naturally, I find them as titillating as those that suggested them do.

I have included some words which I am sure will be known to most if not all of our eccentric and learned readers, but I have included them out of personal pleasure. Such words include **malapropism, panjandrum, psephology, quisling, recidivism, stevedore, Sybaritic, ziggurat** and many others which will probably be known to some of you.

Christopher Foyle
September 2008

Acknowledgements

I would like to acknowledge the help of my daughter Charlotte, who helped me with the preparation and consolidation of the final list and who, together with others, helped me to find many new, unusual words. The others include: Michael Clark, George Courtauld, Sir Peter Duffield, Alex Goldmark, Jill Gunter, Frank Herrmann, Christine Jelleyman, Nick Johnstone, Peter McBarron, Leo McKinstry, Alex Martin, John Julius Norwich, Edward Oakley, Julia Shipton, Miriam Ward, Chris Theo, Christopher Williams, and last but not least the enormously supportive and helpful editorial staff at Chambers Harrap, my publisher.

Note on pronunciations

Part of the enjoyment of collecting unusual words is going on to use them in everyday conversation. Where the pronunciation of a word is not immediately obvious, guidance is included in the note accompanying the entry. Although these notes should be fairly self-explanatory, a list of the letter-combinations used to indicate the different vowel sounds is included below:

a	as in *bat*
ah	as in *far*
ai	as in *mine*
aw	as in *all*
ay	as in *pay*
e	as in *pet*
ee	as in *tee*
i	as in *bid*
o	as in *got*
oh	as in *note*
oo	as in *moon*
ow	as in *house*
oy	as in *boy*
u	as in *bud*
uh	as in *bird*
yoo	as in *tube*

Aa

abalone
noun
an edible shellfish, the sea-ear, especially a richly coloured variety found on the Pacific coast of North America
→ This word is derived from the American Spanish word *abulon*. It is pronounced 'ab-uh-*lone*-ee', with the stress on the third syllable. A word known to many, but pleasing to the ear; it sounds delicious.

abecedarian
noun
1 a learner of the ABC
2 a beginner
3 a teacher of the ABC
4 an Anabaptist of a sect that rejected all learning
→ The word is pronounced 'ay-bee-see-*day*-ri-uhn', with the stress on the fourth syllable.

abibliophobia
noun
the fear or anxiety that one will run out of things to read
→ Those of us that suffer from this affliction compensate by buying a ridiculous amount of books.

abiogenesis
noun
the origination of living by non-living matter; spontaneous generation

&This word was coined by the English biologist T H Huxley in 1870. It is derived from *a-* meaning 'without', *bios* meaning 'life' and *genesis* meaning 'birth'.

aboulia

noun

1 loss of willpower

2 inability to make decisions

&These phenomena are doubtless familiar to many readers, who might take comfort from the fact that they are not modern ailments: this word was first recorded in the middle of the 19th century.

absit

noun

permission to spend one night away from college

&This is a Latin word that literally means 'let him (or her or it) be absent'.

absquatulate

verb

1 to decamp

2 to squat

&This word is used facetiously in American English.

absterge

verb

to wipe; to cleanse; to purge

abyssopelagic

adjective

relating to the deepest regions of the ocean

&This word is derived from Greek *abyssos* meaning 'bottomless' and *pelagos* meaning 'sea'.

acalculia

noun

the inability to make simple mathematical calculations

ᕽ᳎This word is pronounced 'ay-kal-*kyoo*-li-uh', with the stress on the third syllable.

accidie

noun

listlessness; torpor; sloth

ᕽ᳎This word is a variant of 'acedia', which is derived from Greek *a-* meaning 'without' and *kedos* meaning 'care'. Accidie, or sloth, is one of the seven deadly sins in Christian tradition.

accloy

verb

to injure with a horseshoe nail

ᕽ᳎This word is derived from Old French *encloyer*, which is itself derived from Latin *in* meaning 'in' and *clavus* meaning 'a nail'. Unsurprisingly, given its meaning, this word is now obsolete. It is, however, a good one to have ready if you move in equestrian circles.

achromatopsia

noun

total colour-blindness

acock

adverb

defiantly

ᕽ᳎This word is derived from the 'male bird' sense of cock, and relates to its strutting confidence.

acosmism

noun

disbelief in the existence of an eternal world, or of a world distinct from God

acrasia

noun

weakness of will, by which a person acts against usual or expected judgement

acrolith

noun

a wooden statue with stone extremities

    ⇛This word is derived from Greek *akron* meaning 'point' and *lithos* meaning 'stone'. The Colossus of Constantine was an acrolith located in the Basilica of Maxentius in Rome. The head, arms and legs were made of marble, and some of these pieces are still intact.

acushla

noun

an Anglo-Irish word for darling

    ⇛This intimate-sounding term of endearment has an anatomical etymology. It is derived from Irish *cuisle* meaning 'vein'.

Adamite

noun

1 a descendant of Adam
2 a person who goes about naked, especially a member of a 2nd-century sect in North Africa

adunc

adjective

hooked

    ⇛This word is derived from Latin *ad* meaning 'to' and *uncus* meaning 'a hook'.

aestivate

verb

to pass the summer in a state of torpor

    ⇛This word is derived from Latin *aestivus* meaning 'of Summer'. It is the opposite of the much more familiar hibernate, which is derived from Latin *hibernus* meaning 'of Winter'.

affluenza

noun

a malaise said to affect affluent young people, characterized by feelings of guilt and isolation

    ⇛Some of us seem to be suffering from this today.

after-clap

noun

an unexpected sequel, after an affair is supposed to be at an end

&❧This is an archaic word.

agelast

noun

a person who never laughs

&❧This word is derived from Greek *a-* meaning 'without' and *gelaein* meaning 'to laugh'. It is pronounced '*aj*-i-last', with the stress on the first syllable.

agerasia

noun

a youthful appearance in an old person

&❧Derived from Greek *a-* meaning 'not' and *geras* meaning 'old age', this word first appeared in the 18th century with the meaning 'not growing old'. In the superficial noughties, the meaning of this word now focuses on appearance, that is the *appearance* of not growing old.

agrom

noun

a disease of the tongue in which it becomes rough and cracked

&❧This word comes from Gujarati *agrun*.

ahimsa

noun

the duty of sparing animal life; non-violence

&❧This Sanskrit word describes a belief that is important in Buddhism, Hinduism and Jainism.

akathisia

noun

a psychological condition characterized by agitation and a frequent desire to alter the posture

&❧This is derived from Greek *a-* meaning 'without' and *kathizein* meaning 'to sit down'.

alembroth or sal alembroth
noun
an alchemist's word for mercury ammonium chloride, also known as 'salt of wisdom'

allantoid
adjective
sausage-shaped

amathophobia
noun
a fear of dust

ambergris
noun
a strongly scented ash-grey substance, originating in the intestines of the spermaceti whale and used in the manufacture of perfumes
  ఈ This word is pronounced '*am*-buhr-grees', with the stress on the first syllable.

ambigram
noun
a graphic design of a word in which the word appears the same after the design has undergone some kind of movement, such as reversal or inversion

ambulacrum
noun
a radial band in the shell of an echinoderm, bearing rows of pores through which the tube-feet protrude

ammophilous
adjective
sand-loving
  ఈ This word is pronounced '*am*-*mof*-il-uhs', with the stress on the second syllable.

amplexus
noun
the clasping of the female of certain amphibians by the male as part of the mating process

amrita
noun
the drink of the Hindu gods
    ह➤This is derived from a Sanskrit word meaning 'immortal'.

anadiplosis
noun
the repetition of an important word or, sometimes, phrase for rhetorical effect
    ह➤An example of anadiplosis can be found in the Bible at Romans, chapter 5, verses 3 to 5: '...but we glory in tribulations also; knowing that tribulation worketh patience; and patience, experience; and experience, hope: and hope maketh not ashamed'.

anaphora
noun
the rhetorical device of beginning successive sentences, lines, etc with the same word or phrase
    ह➤A well-known example of anaphora can be found in the Bible in Paul's Epistle to the Philippians, chapter 4, verse 8: 'Finally, brethren, whatsoever things are true, whatsoever things are honest, whatsoever things are just, whatsoever things are pure, whatsoever things are lovely, whatsoever things are of good report; if there be any virtue, and if there be any praise, think on these things'.

anaxiphilia
noun
the act of falling in love with someone unsuitable, especially someone considered unworthy

ancon
noun
1 the elbow

2 (architecture) a console to support a door cornice
3 a breed of sheep with very short legs

> ≷This word is derived from Greek *ankon* meaning 'a bend'. It is obvious
> how this would apply to an elbow. The architectural 'ancon' has a bend
> in it. The legs of the ancon sheep, as well as being short, were crooked.
> Hence, three things that, at first sight, have little in common, are
> connected by meaning, and end up sharing one name.

ancress

noun
1 a woman who has withdrawn from the world, especially for
religious reasons
2 a recluse

> ≷One of the best-known ancresses or anchoresses was Dame Julian of
> Norwich, whose mystical visions inspired her work *Sixteen Revelations
> of Divine Love*. This book, which was published in about 1393, was the
> first book by a woman published in the English language.

andrology

noun
the branch of medicine which deals with functions and diseases
specific to males

anemophobia

noun
the fear of wind or draughts

anencephalic

adjective
without a brain

> ≷This word is pronounced 'an-en-sef-*al*-ik', with the stress on the fourth
> syllable.

anepigraphous or anepigraphic

adjective
not carrying an inscription or epigraph

angels' share
noun
the amount of a spirit lost in the cask through evaporation

anhedonia
noun
1 the inability to feel pleasure
2 the loss of interest in formerly pleasurable pursuits

anile
adjective
1 old-womanish
2 imbecile

antelucan
adjective
(archaic, literary) before dawn or daylight

anthelion
noun
1 a luminous coloured ring seen on a cloud or fog bank opposite the sun
2 a white spot on the parhelic circle (a luminous band parallel to the horizon) seen opposite the sun
    This word is pronounced 'an-*thee*-li-uhn', with the stress on the second syllable. It is derived from Greek *anti* meaning 'opposite' and *helios* meaning 'the sun'.

Anthropocene
noun
the present geological age, starting roughly at the time of the industrial revolution, considered as the period when human activities started having an impact on the earth's environment
    The term 'Anthropocene' was coined by Paul Crutzen, a Dutch chemist who won the Nobel Prize in Chemistry in 1995.

anthropomorphosis
noun
a transformation into human shape
> ❧This word is pronounced 'an-throp-oh-morf-*oh*-zis', with the stress on the fifth syllable.

antigram
noun
an anagram in which the new word or phrase created has the opposite meaning to the original word or phrase
> ❧Some examples of antigrams are 'united' and 'untied', and 'funeral' and 'real fun'.

anti-guggler
noun
a small tube inserted into a container, to allow the liquid content to be poured out without causing a gurgling noise or spluttering

antilog or antilogarithm
noun
a number of which a particular number is the logarithm

antinomian
adjective
relating to the belief that Christians are emancipated by the gospel from the obligation to keep the moral law, faith alone being necessary

antinomy
noun
1 a contradiction between two beliefs or conclusions, both of which are reasonable in themselves; a paradox
2 a conflict between two laws or authorities
> ❧This word is pronounced 'an-*tin*-oh-mi', with the stress on the second syllable.

antithalian
adjective
opposed to mirth or fun

ⅾThalia is the Greek muse of comedy, who is often portrayed in art holding a comic mask.

aphaeresis
noun
the omission of a letter, sound or syllable at the beginning of a word
ⅾ'Knife' is an example of aphaeresis. In Old and Middle English, the initial 'k' sound was pronounced. This was gradually lost, leaving the modern pronunciation 'naif'.

aphesis
noun
the gradual and unintentional loss of an unaccented vowel at the beginning of a word
ⅾThis is a particular type of aphaeresis. An example of this is 'esquire', which gradually lost its unstressed first syllable, leaving us with 'squire'. Another example of this is the development of 'escapegoat' into 'scapegoat'.

apocatastasis
noun
1 the final restitution of all things at the appearance of the Messiah, to the final conversion and salvation of all created beings, including the devil and his angels
2 the process of return to previous or normal condition

apocolocynotosis
noun
the process of being turned into a pumpkin; pumpkinification
ⅾAs many of us have a fear of this, it is useful to know its proper name. It is a Latinized Greek word, the title of a satirical work by Seneca the Younger on the Roman Emperor Claudius. Roman emperors were deified on death, a process known as *apotheosis*, from *apo-* expressing 'completeness' and *theos* meaning 'a god'. The Greek word for pumpkin or gourd is *kolokynthis*, so the process of becoming a pumpkin combines *apo-* and *kolokynthis*. This is my family's favourite word, not because of Cinderella, but because our golden retriever is called Pumpkin.

apocope
noun
the cutting off of the last sound or syllable of a word
  ~Some examples of apocope are 'doc' for 'doctor' and 'sarge' for 'sergeant'.

apolaustic
adjective
devoted to the search for enjoyment

apotropaic
adjective
turning aside (or intended to turn aside) evil

apposite
adjective
1 apt; appropriate; well-chosen
2 expressed well

apricate
verb
to bask in the sun
  ~This is a rare word, but worth using in place of its more pedestrian
    synonym 'sunbathe'.

apsaras
noun
1 (Hindu mythology) a divine water sprite
2 one of these beings represented as a voluptuous female figure in
Hindu temple carvings, paintings, etc

aquose
adjective
watery, aqueous

arame
noun
a type of edible seaweed, looking like black bootlaces

ई➤This Japanese word is pronounced 'uh-*rah*-mi', with the stress on the second syllable.

arcane
adjective
1 mysterious; secret; known only by a few
2 difficult to understand
ई➤This word is derived from Latin *arcere* meaning 'to shut up', which itself comes from *arca* meaning 'a chest'.

arctophile
noun
a lover or collector of teddy bears
ई➤The first part of this word is from Greek *arktos* meaning 'a bear'. This Greek word is also the origin of 'arctic', via Latin *arcticus* meaning 'of the northern constellation of the Great Bear'.

ariolater
noun
a soothsayer, a fortune teller

arithmophobia
noun
the fear of numbers

armamentarium
noun
the collective equipment, medicines, etc, that are available to a doctor
ई➤If you are wondering if this word is related to 'armament' you are correct. In Latin, *armamentarium* is literally 'an arsenal or armoury'. It is interesting how often the vocabulary of warfare is used in medical contexts: we *fight* disease, illnesses can be *vanquished*, and people win or lose their *battles* with cancer.

armozeen
noun
a kind of taffeta or plain silk, usually black, used for clerical gowns

aroynt
verb
(archaic) to drive or frighten away
> 'Aroynt' or 'aroint' will be familiar to those who have read *Macbeth*. In Act I, Scene iii, the first witch describes an encounter with a sailor's wife who tells her 'Aroint thee, witch!' meaning 'Begone, witch!'

arquebusade
noun
a lotion for shotgun wounds
> An 'arquebus' or 'harquebus' is a portable long-barrelled gun.

arundinaceous
noun
of or like a reed

aspectabund
adjective
having a face that shows emotions clearly

autarchy
noun
absolute power; autocracy

autocoprophagy
noun
the act of eating one's own faeces

autogram
noun
a sentence that describes its own content
> An example of an autogram is 'This sentence appears in *Foyle's Further Philavery*'.

autolatry
noun
the worship of oneself

☙This useful word is pronounced 'or-*tol*-uh-tre', with the stress on the second syllable.

autoscopy
noun
(psychology) hallucination of an image of one's body

aventurine
noun
1 a brown spangled kind of Venetian glass
2 a kind of quartz containing spangles of mica or haematite
adjective
shimmering or spangled, eg of certain kinds of feldspar or sealing wax

☙This word comes from Italian *avventura* meaning 'chance' because of the accidental discovery of the glass.

azolla
noun
a type of small floating fern

Bb

badderlock

noun

(Scots) an edible seaweed of the genus *Alaria*

    șThis seaweed is also known as 'balderlocks', which reinforces the belief
that the name is derived from *Balder's locks*, after the Norse god Balder.

baetyl

noun

a magical or holy meteoric stone

baffle jelly

noun

a deposit which builds up in air-conditioning plants and hot water
systems of large buildings, and provides a breeding ground for
disease

bagarre

noun

a scuffle, a brawl, a rumpus

Bairam

noun

the Turkish name for the Muslim festivals of Eid al-Adha (the
Greater Bairam) and Eid al-Fitr (the Lesser Bairam)

Balaam

noun

1 a prophet who strives to mislead, like Balaam in the Bible (Numbers, chapters 22 to 24)

2 unimportant paragraphs kept in readiness to fill up a newspaper

  ☙It has been suggested that the connection between these senses is that the unimportant paragraphs of newspaper filler appear to be the writings of an idiot, comparable to the words spoken by Balaam's donkey. In newspaper offices the 'Balaam-box' or 'Balaam-basket' is the place where these filler items are kept ready for use when required.

balibuntal

noun

1 a type of fine, closely woven straw

2 a hat made of this straw

  ☙This word is derived from *Baliuag*, a town in the Philippines, and Tagalog *buntal*, meaning 'the straw of the talipot palm'.

bangster

noun

(obsolete Scots)

1 a violent person

2 a braggart

3 a victor

banjax

verb

1 to ruin, destroy

2 to thwart

barbate

adjective

bearing a hairy tuft

barp

noun

(Scots) a mound or cairn

bartavel
noun
the red-legged partridge

bashment
noun
1 a sense of confusion caused by a sudden surprise
2 a feeling of shame
3 a type of reggae with a beat that is faster than usual
ɞ➥It is interesting to see that this Middle English word, which is rarely
used in its original meanings, developed another sense at the end of the
20th century.

bastarda
noun
a typeface used during the 14th and 15th centuries

bastinado
verb
to beat with a baton or stick, especially on the soles of the feet

bathophobia
noun
a morbid fear of falling from a high place
ɞ➥The origin of this word is the Greek *bathos* meaning 'depth'. In case you
were wondering, a morbid fear of baths or bathing' is 'ablutophobia'.

bathykolpian
adjective
having a large bosom with a deep cleavage

batology
noun
the study of brambles

bausond

adjective

(obsolete, Scots and Northern English) of animals, having white spots, especially on the forehead, or a white stripe down the face

bawcock

noun

a fine fellow

> ತ►This Shakespearean word can be found in *Twelfth Night, The Winter's Tale*, and *Henry V*, which contains this description of the king himself: 'The king's a bawcock, and heart of gold, a lad of life, an imp of fame'.

beadledom

noun

stupid officiousness

> ತ►The 'beadle' is the name for a number of office bearers in different organizations: a vice-chancellor's mace bearer at Oxford and Cambridge Universities; formerly, a parish officer with the power to punish minor offenders; and, within the Church of Scotland, the church officer who attends the minister.

beadsman

noun

(Scots) a licensed beggar

beblubbered

adjective

disfigured by weeping

> ತ►This wonderfully descriptive word came into use in the 16th century, and really deserves a revival.

bedaggle

verb

to dirty by dragging along the wet ground

> ತ►This word predates its much commoner synonym 'bedraggle' by almost 150 years.

belcher

noun

a neckerchief, especially one with blue-centred white spots on a dark blue background

> ঙ▸This is named after the English bare-knuckle boxer Jem Belcher (1781-1811), one of the most successful and admired boxers of his time. He popularized this style of neckerchief, which eventually took his name. There are numerous examples of clothing items taking their name from the famous people who wore them: Prince Albert frock coat, Bonnie Prince Charlie jacket, Gandhi cap, Nehru jacket, Mao suit, cardigan, wellington boot, Jackie Howe, Chesterfield coat and Davy Crockett hat. Articles of clothing named after fictional characters include Mother Hubbard, tam-o-shanter, Juliet cap and Dolly Varden.

Benedick or Benedict

noun

a name for a newly married man, especially if formerly a confirmed bachelor

> ঙ▸This comes from the character of Benedick in Shakespeare's *Much Ado about Nothing*.

benet

noun

an exorcist, the third of the four lesser orders in the Roman Catholic Church

> ঙ▸The other three orders are 'porter', 'lector' and 'acolyte'.

benthonic

adjective

living on the bottom of the sea

benthoscope

noun

a submersible sphere from which to study deep-sea life

besom

noun

(Scots) a term of reproach, especially for a woman, implying slatternliness, laziness, impudence, or unscrupulous energy

bibcock

noun

a tap with a downturned nozzle

bibelot

noun

a knick-knack

ஃThis word is pronounced '*beeb*-loh', with the stress on the first syllable.

bibliomania

noun

1 a mania for collecting or possessing books
2 a love of books

ஃThere is no cure for this affliction other than self-gratification.

bibliophobia

noun

a hatred of books

bilbo

noun

a rapier or sword

ஃThis is named after the Spanish city of Bilbao.

billingsgate

noun

foul and abusive language

ஃThe London fish market was located in the Billingsgate district of the city for the best part of 300 years, until the early 1980s. The sometimes colourful language of the fish traders gave rise to this meaning of the word, a meaning echoed in the term 'fishwife'.

bilocation
noun
the ability to be in two places simultaneously
&❧Many wives believe that their husbands should have this ability.

binnacle
noun
the casing in which a ship's compass is kept

biosystematics
noun
the study of relationships of organisms and of laws of classification

bismer
verb
to treat scornfully; to mock

bitter end
noun
1 (nautical) the end of the cable wound round a post (a *bitt*)
2 the end of a task, however long-drawn-out or difficult

blatherskite
noun
(dialect) a garrulous talker of nonsense

blether
verb
1 to talk garrulous nonsense
2 to chat; to gossip
noun
1 a person who blethers
2 a chat
&❧This word had fallen out of use in Standard British English but remains
common in Scots, in various British dialects, and in the United States.

bleupsy
adjective
(Orkney) fat; obese

bloviate
verb
(US slang) to speak arrogantly or pompously
&This useful word has been created from 'blow' meaning 'to boast', and the pseudo-Latinate suffix 'viate'.

blurbist
noun
a person who writes copy for the cover of a book
&'Blurb', which is the complimentary description found on the jacket of a book, is believed to have been coined by the American author Gelett Burgess.

bohunk
noun
(US slang) a Slav or Hungarian, esp an unskilled labourer; the language of such a labourer

bolk
noun
a belch

bombardon
noun
the bass tuba

boodle
noun
1 counterfeit money
2 money obtained by political or official corruption
&This word possibly comes from Dutch *boedel* meaning 'property'.

boomslang
noun
a venomous tree snake of south and east Africa

boondocks
plural noun
(US)
1 wild or remote country
2 a dull provincial place
> ࣳ⮞This comes from Tagalog *bundok* meaning 'a mountain'.

boondoggle
noun
(US)
1 a Scout's plaited cord of varicoloured leather strips
2 an article of simple handcraft
3 work, or a task, of little or no practical value, especially work officially provided as a palliative for unemployment

bootikin
noun
(obsolete)
1 a boot or mitten for the gouty
2 an infant's legging
3 (Scots) a boot used for torture
> ࣳ⮞Here is one innocent-sounding word for three very different things. The first is an object to ease the discomfort of gout. The second is an item of clothing to keep a baby warm. And the third is an instrument for creating unbearable pressure on the foot and lower leg in order to inflict agony on the victim. Bootikin – what could sound more innocuous?

bottine
noun
1 a high boot
2 a half-boot
3 a lady's boot
4 a small boot

boustrophedon
adjective
(of ancient writing) alternately from right to left and from left to right
  👄This Greek word means 'turning like ploughing oxen'. It is pronounced 'boo-strof-*ee*-don', with the stress on the third syllable.

boyg
noun
1 an ogre
2 an obstacle or problem difficult to get to grips with
  👄This unusual-sounding word comes from Norwegian.

brachygraph
noun
certain old systems of shorthand

brasero
noun
1 a brazier
2 a place for burning criminals or heretics

braw
adjective
(Scots)
1 fine, splendid
2 dressed finely
  👄This variant of 'brave' features in that (allegedly) typically Scots saying, 'It's a braw bricht moonlicht nicht'.

bream
verb
to clean (a ship's bottom) by burning off seaweed, shells, etc

brever
noun
a book-keeper or record-keeper

Briarean
adjective
relating to Briareus, a hundred-handed giant in Greek mythology;
many-handed

bricole
noun
a medieval military catapult for hurling stones

brio
noun
liveliness, vivacity, spirit
> ₰This is the Italian word for 'liveliness' or 'vigour' and English speakers
> would be most likely to encounter it in the musical instruction *con brio*
> which means 'with vivacity'.

broch
noun
1 a dry-built circular tower of the late Iron Age, common in Scotland
2 a luminous ring around the moon

Brocken spectre
noun
the shadow of an observer, enlarged and often surrounded by
coloured lights, thrown onto a bank of cloud, a phenomenon
sometimes encountered on mountain tops
> ₰This phenomenon can be seen on any bank of clouds, but it has been
> so often witnessed upon the *Brocken*, a peak in the Harz Mountains of
> Germany, that it has taken its name from it.

bromidrosis
noun
the secretion of ill-smelling sweat
> ₰This affliction, which is also known as osmidrosis, takes its name from
> Greek *bromos* meaning 'a stink'.

Brompton stock
noun
a biennial variety of the stock plant *Matthiola incana*

   ❧This plant, also known as gillyflower, was first developed in Brompton Park in London. It takes its botanical name, *Matthiola incana*, from Matthiole, a 16th-century botanist and doctor, who was personal physician to Maximilian I of Austria.

brouhaha
noun
fuss, excitement, clamour, or an instance of this

brummagem
noun
1 (with a capital) the city of Birmingham
2 a thing made in Birmingham, especially something showy and worthless
adjective
showy and worthless; sham, counterfeit

   ❧This variant name for Birmingham dates back to the 17th century, and is the source of the current informal names for the city (Brum) and its inhabitants (Brummies). Since that time the city has been a centre for the production of all manner of metal objects, including swords, cutlery, buckles, buttons, snuff boxes, trinkets and costume jewellery. The sheer quantity of objects produced meant that some were of inferior quality, and this led to *brummagem* having a meaning of 'counterfeit' or 'worthless'. This unenviable reputation worried the city's silversmiths, who campaigned for Birmingham to have its own assay office. They were successful and the Birmingham Assay Office with its anchor mark went a long way to establishing the city as a hugely important centre of fine silverware.

brumous
adjective
foggy, wintry

buccal
adjective
1 of, towards or relating to the cheek
2 relating to the mouth, oral

buddle
noun
a sloping container for washing ore

bugaboo
noun
1 a bogy, or object of terror
2 a cause of anxiety
> A 'bug' is an obsolete name for an object of terror. It comes from Middle English *bugge*, which may itself be derived from Welsh *bwg* meaning 'a hobgoblin'.

bull-beggar
noun
(dialect) a hobgoblin

bullfist
noun
the puffball fungus

bullyrag or ballyrag
verb
1 to assail with abusive language or horseplay
2 to badger, to intimidate

bumble-puppy
noun
1 the old game of nine-holes
2 unscientific whist or bridge
3 a racket game in which a string is wound round a post by hitting a slung ball or bag

bummel

noun

1 a stroll
2 a leisurely journey

   ∾'Bummel' is a German word. Jerome K Jerome's sequel to *Three Men in a Boat* was *Three Men on the Bummel*, which relates the adventures of J (the narrator), Harris and George on a cycling tour of the Black Forest. It was used as a school text book in Germany for many years.

buskin

noun

1 a high thick-soled boot worn in ancient times by actors in tragedy
2 tragedy as a dramatic genre

busyness or business

noun

a collective name for a group of ferrets

buttock-mail

noun

(Scots) the fine formerly exacted by the church in commutation of sitting on the stool of repentance

   ∾The stool of repentance was formerly a means of punishing wrong-doers within the Church of Scotland. Those who had offended in some way were obliged to sit on an elevated seat in church, in full view of the congregation. The minister would then chastise them publicly. Through buttock-mail, an offender could avoid the humiliation of the stool of repentance by paying a fine instead. *Mail* is a Scots word meaning 'a payment'.

Cc

cabré
adjective
1 (in heraldry) rearing
2 (of an aeroplane) flying upturned with the tail down

cachalot
noun
the sperm whale

cachinnate
verb
(formal or literary) to laugh loudly

cacoethes
noun
1 a bad habit or itch
2 an uncontrollable urge or desire
3 an itch or intense longing
    This word comes from Greek *kakos* meaning 'bad' and *ethos* meaning 'a habit'. It can be used in combination with other words, so *cacoethes loquendi* is 'a mania for talking, especially for giving speeches' and *cacoethes scribendi* is 'a mania for writing or getting things into print'. It is pronounced 'kak-oh-*ee*-theez', with the stress on the third syllable.

cacogastric
adjective
of or relating to an upset stomach

cacography
noun
bad handwriting or spelling

cacology
noun
a bad choice of words or faulty pronunciation

cacotopia
noun
a state, imaginary or otherwise, in which everything is as bad as it can possibly be
  ⭢The opposite of 'utopia' (where everything is as good as it can possibly be), 'cacotopia' is the same as 'dystopia', but is nothing like as commonly used.

cakewalk
noun
1 a dance developed from a prancing movement once performed by African-Americans in competition for a cake
2 something accomplished with supreme ease

caliginous
adjective
(archaic) dim, obscure, dark

callaloo or callalloo
noun
a dark green Caribbean soup or stew made from a green leaf vegetable such as amaranth, dasheen or sometimes spinach, with varying ingredients including okra, coconut milk, onion and crab legs
  ⭢*Callaloo* is a Jamaican name for 'amaranth'.

calligram
noun
a design that uses the letters of a word to illustrate the word's meaning
> ❧An example of a calligram would be the word 'stretch' when the letters have all been pulled or stretched out widely.

calvary
noun
an experience of intense mental suffering
> ❧In the New Testament, Calvary was the place near Jerusalem where Jesus was crucified.

calvities
noun
baldness

camaïeu
noun
1 a cameo
2 a painting in monochrome, or in simple colours not imitating nature
3 a style of printing pictures producing the effect of pencil-drawing
4 a literary work or play that is monotonous or lacks interest

cameline
noun
a material made from camel hair

capernoity
(Scots)
noun
the head
adjective
1 peevish, irritable
2 capricious
3 drunk, giddy

&The Scots poet Robert Fergusson wrote in his poem '*The Daft-Days*':
'When fou we're sometimes capernoity'.

carboy

noun

a large glass or plastic bottle, with basketwork or other casing, used
for containing or transporting dangerous chemicals

&This word is derived from Persian *qarabah*.

carminative

noun

a medicine that prevents or relieves flatulence

adjective

expelling or relieving flatulence

carriwitchet

noun

1 a quip

2 a quibble

catafalque

noun

a temporary tomb-like structure used in funeral ceremonies and
processions

&This word has come into English from Italian *catafalco*. Hardly a word
one would need to use every day, it enjoyed something of a revival in
April 2002 when the coffin of Queen Elizabeth, the Queen Mother,
lay in state on a catafalque in Westminster Hall. The coverage of this
occasion was the first time many people had heard the word.

cataplexy

noun

1 a condition of immobility induced by extreme emotion, such as
shock

2 a physical state resembling death, adopted by some animals to
discourage predators

catenary

noun

the curve formed by a flexible cord, hanging freely between two points of support, and acted on by no other force than gravity

caterwaul

noun

the shriek or cry emitted by a domestic cat, especially when in heat

verb

1 to make such a noise

2 to make any discordant sound similar to this, especially loud and tuneless singing

3 (archaic) to behave lasciviously

4 to quarrel like cats

cattalo

noun

a cross between the bison ('buffalo') and the domestic cow

    ➥This takes its name from 'cattle' and 'buffalo'. It is also known as the 'beefalo', from 'beef' and 'buffalo'. Animal interbreeding has given rise to many interesting new words to describe the resultant offspring: mimophant (a mimosa with an elephant); liger (a lion with a female tiger); tigon (a male tiger with a lioness); zonkey, zeedonk, zebronkey and deebra (a zebra with a donkey); zorse (a zebra stallion with a horse mare); cama (a camel with a llama); and numerous dog hybrids, both deliberate and accidental, such as labradoodle, jackadoodle, cockapoo, dorgi, cavapoo, puggle and schnoodle.

ceromancy

noun

divination by dropping melted wax in water

    ➥Now believed to be used by hedge fund managers.

cete

noun

a collective noun for a group of badgers

    ➥This is possibly derived from Latin *coetus* meaning 'an assembly'.

chatoyant
adjective
(of gems, birds' plumage, etc) with a changing lustre, iridescent, shimmering
  ᔫThis anglicised pronunciation of this word is 'shat-*oy*-uhnt', with the stress on the second syllable.

chewet
noun
(obsolete) a pie or pudding of miscellaneous chopped meats

chiffchaff
noun
a small European warbler, *Phylloscopus collybita*
  ᔫThe bird's name is an imitation of its call.

chincherinchee
noun
a liliaceous South African plant, with dense, conical spikes of cup-shaped white flowers.
  ᔫThis is another imitative name: it is said to represent the sound of its flower stalks rubbing together in the wind. And here is another interesting fact about chincherinchee: it is the only word in English that has one letter occurring once, two letters occurring twice, and three letters occurring three times.

chott or shott
noun
in North Africa and the Middle East, a shallow watercourse or lake that tends to dry up in certain seasons

chrestomathy
noun
an anthology of choice or literary passages, usually used by students in the learning of a foreign language
  ᔫThis is derived from Greek *chrestos* meaning 'useful' and *mathein* meaning 'to know'.

chrysophilite

noun

a lover of gold

> ॐ➤This word is pronounced 'kris-*of*-fil-ait', with stress on the second syllable.

chthonian

adjective

1 relating to the earth or the underworld and the deities inhabiting it

2 ghostly

> ॐ➤Derived from Greek *chthonos* meaning 'the ground', this word is pronounced '*thoh*-ni-uhn', with the stress on the first syllable.

cicerone

noun

a person who shows and explains the curiosities of a place to visitors and sightseers; a guide

> ॐ➤This name comes from Marcus Tullius *Cicero* (died 43 BC), the Roman statesman, philosopher and orator, presumably as a recognition of his erudition and eloquence.

cicisbeo

noun

the acknowledged lover of a married woman

> ॐ➤From Italian, this is pronounced 'chee-cheez-*bay*-oh', with the stress on the third syllable.

cinquasept

noun

a visit to one's lover between the hours of five and seven o'clock

cippus

noun

the stocks, a device for holding a delinquent by the ankles, and often wrists

circumambient
adjective
going round about, emcompassing

clamjamphrie
noun
(Scots) rubbish; nonsense
&ntThe origin of this wonderfully expressive word is unknown.

clanjandering
noun
(Essex) gossip, especially that of women
&ntA wonderfully onomatopoeic, Essex word.

clapperdudgeon
noun
someone born as a beggar to beggar parents

clart
noun
(Scots and Northern English) mud; dirt

cleg
noun
a gadfly, a horse-fly

clem
verb
to starve
&ntThe adjective *clemmed* meaning 'very hungry' is still used in a number of English dialects.

clepsydra
noun
an instrument for measuring time by the trickling of water, a water clock

clerihew

noun

a humorous poem that sums up the life and character of some notable person in two short couplets

> ઠ•This form of comic verse was invented by the English humorist Edmund Clerihew Bentley (1875-1956). A clerihew must contain the subject's name in the first line, be four lines in length, consist of two sets of rhyming couplets, have third and fourth lines longer than the first and second, and take a whimsical rather than cynical view of its subject. Bentley's first clerihew is reputed to have been written when he was a schoolboy:
>
>> Sir Humphry Davy
>> Abominated gravy.
>> He lived in the odium
>> Of having discovered sodium.

clinkstone

noun

a fine-grained intermediate igneous rock that rings when struck by a hammer; phonolite

clinophobia

noun

a fear of going to bed

clinquant

adjective

tinselly; glittering with gold or tinsel

clishmaclaver

noun

(Scots) gossip

> ઠ•In Scots, an internet chatroom is a 'clishmaclaver room'.

cloop

noun

the sound of drawing a cork from a bottle

> ઠ•It is not hard to understand where this onomatopoeic word came from.

cloot

noun

(Scots) a cloth

→The English proverb that warns against removing one's undergarments too early in the year is rendered in Scots as 'N'er cast a cloot till May be oot'. A Scottish culinary delicacy is the clootie dumpling: a suet pudding containing currants and raisins, and boiled in a cloth or *cloot*.

clowder

noun

a collective name for a number of cats

→This rare word is a variant of 'clutter'.

coleopterist

noun

a person who studies and collects beetles

collieshangie

noun

(Scots)

1 a noisy wrangling

2 an uproar

3 a disturbance

comedogenic

adjective

causing blackheads

comicar

noun

someone who write comedies

comstock

noun

a rich source of ore

→This takes its name from the Comstock Lode discovered in the Virginia Range in Nevada in (it is believed) 1857. It was the first major deposit of silver ore found in the US and was a source of a fabulous amount of both silver and gold. The lode was apparently discovered by two brothers, Ethan and Hosea Grosh, and when they both died prematurely an associate, Henry T P *Comstock*, staked a claim for the area.

comstockery

noun

vigorous censorship or suppression of literary or artistic material considered to be salacious

> ੬►This word was coined by George Bernard Shaw after Anthony *Comstock* (1844-1915), an American politician and activist who was responsible for the introduction of the Comstock Act in 1873, which outlawed the delivery of material considered lewd or obscene. This definition of obscene was broad, and it included anatomy text books and information on contraception.

conchology

noun

the study of molluscs and their shells

concinnity

noun

1 harmony
2 congruity
3 elegance

> ੬►This word comes from Latin *concinnus* meaning 'well-adjusted'.

constuprate

verb

(obsolete) to ravish

contiguity

noun

the quality or state of being adjoining, touching, near or next to in space or time

contumelious
adjective
haughtily insolent

coprolalia
noun
obsessive or repetitive use of obscene language, eg as a characteristic
of Tourette's syndrome
　⛯This word is derived from Greek *kopros* meaning 'dung' and *lalia*
　　meaning 'talk'.

corrigendum
noun
something which requires correction
plural noun
corrigenda corrections to be made in a book

coscinomancy
noun
an ancient mode of divination by a sieve and pair of shears

coulrophia
noun
a morbid fear of clowns
　⛯The number of films that feature a scary clown would suggest that this
　　phobia is deeply embedded in the Western psyche. Indeed, there is
　　something about the hideously painted face that causes many to shrink
　　instinctively in horror. Recent research has come up with the not-so-
　　surprising conclusion that clown visits to sick children in hospital have
　　a detrimental rather than a beneficial effect.

couthie
adjective
(Scots)
1 friendly, kindly
2 comfortable, snug
　⛯This word is probably derived from Old English *cuth* meaning 'known':
　　something or someone that is known or familiar to us is likely to appear

friendly and to make us feel comfortable. Something unknown or unfamiliar – *uncuth* – can seem threatening and strange, or 'uncouth'.

cowpat roulette or cow bingo
noun
a game in which villagers bet on which plot of land will be the first to receive a cow's calling card

crambo
noun
a game in which one player gives a word to which another finds a rhyme
> ຂະThis term is believed to be derived from Latin *crambe repetita* meaning 'cabbage that is served up again'.

crapehanger
noun
a pessimist
> ຂະCrape was the fabric of mourning in the past, either in the form of the clothes themselves, or in a band to trim a hat or be worn as an armband. Someone who is eternally pessimistic and miserable might seem as to be in a state of perpetual mourning, hence a 'crapehanger'.

craquelure
noun
1 the fine cracking that occurs in the varnish or pigment of old paintings
2 this effect or pattern

crepance
noun
a wound on a horse's hind ankle joint, caused by the shoe of the other hind-foot

crepitus
noun
(medical) the grating sound produced when an arthritic joint is moved or when a fractured bone is disturbed

crinigerous
adjective
hairy

crinkum-crankum
noun
a whimsical word for something that is full of intricate twists and
turns

crithomancy
noun
divination by strewing meal over sacrificial animals

crizzling
noun
fine cracks in the surface of glass, caused by a fault in its chemical
composition

crotal
noun
1 a lichen used for dyeing
2 the colour of this lichen; golden-brown

crubeen
noun
a pig's trotter, as food
> This is derived from Irish *cruibin*, a diminutive of *crub* meaning 'a
> hoof'. It can be pronounced 'kroo-*been*' or '*kroo*-been', with the stress
> on either the second or the first syllable. This seems to me one of those
> occasions where the word and the thing it represents seem to match
> perfectly.

cruciverbalist
noun
a crossword addict
> Created from Latin *crux* meaning 'cross' and *verbum* meaning 'word',
> this word is a coinage of the late 20th century, probably meant to

appear much older, and probably intended as a joke for the amusement of cruciverbalists themselves.

crwth

noun

the crowd, an old Welsh stringed instrument, four of its six strings played with a bow, two plucked by the thumb

  ❧A word to delight the aforementioned cruciverbalists, *crwth* is a Welsh term meaning 'a hollow protuberance' or 'a fiddle'.

cryptozoology

noun

the study and attempted discovery of creatures, such as the Loch Ness Monster, that are generally regarded as mythical

  ❧Animals proven to exist include the okapi, mountain gorilla, coelacanth, megamouth shark, giant squid and Vu Quang ox of Vietnam. Animals whose existence is as yet unproven include hominids or apes such as the Yeti, Almas, Sasquatch or Bigfoot and Yowie.

cubit

noun

an old measure, the length of the arm from the elbow to the tip of the middle finger, from 18 to 22 inches

cum-twang

noun

(obsolete) a term of contempt or abuse

cunctation

noun

delay, procrastination

cunctator

noun

someone who delays or procrastinates.

curmurring
noun
a rumbling sound, especially that made in the bowels by flatulence

curvicaudate
adjective
having a crooked tail

cybernate
verb
to control (a manufacturing process, etc) by means of a computer
   The *cyber-* prefix is a back formation from 'cybernetics', which is derived from Greek *kybernetes* meaning 'a steersman'. Cyber- is used to denote computers or computer networks, especially the internet, and it has generated many words in recent years including *cybercafé, cybercrime, cybernaut, cyberpet, cyberphobia, cyberpunk, cybersex, cyberslacking, cyberspace, cybersquatting, cyberstalking* and *cyberterrorist.*

cymotrichous
adjective
wavy-haired
   This is pronounced 'sai-*mo*-tri-kuhs', with the stress on the second syllable.

cynophilia
noun
love of dogs
   The Greek word for dog is *kynos*, while the Latin is *canis*. 'Cynophilia' and 'canophilia' are therefore the same thing.

Dd

dacryoma
noun
a stoppage of the tear duct

dag
noun
1 a dirt-clotted tuft of wool on a sheep
2 (Australian informal) a scruffy, untidy, slovenly person
3 (Australian informal) a person who is socially awkward or graceless

dancette
noun
1 (in heraldry) a zigzag or indented line or figure
2 the chevron or zigzag moulding common in Romanesque architecture

> ৯A first look at this word might lead one to believe it is related to 'dance'. However, that is not the case. It is derived from Old French *dent* or *dant* meaning 'a tooth', which itself comes from Latin *dens*, and it therefore related to 'dentist', 'dental' and 'denture'.

dandy-horse
noun
an early bicycle without pedals, driven by kicking the ground

darkle
verb
(literary) to grow dark
&This verb is a back formation from the adjective and adverb 'darkling' meaning 'in the dark'.

dayfelly
noun
(Orkney) a cloud of white mist lying in a depression

deasil, deasoil, deiseal, deisheal or deasiul
(Scots)
adverb
in the direction of the sun's apparent revolution; sunwise
noun
a sunwise motion
&From Gaelic *deiseil*, this is the opposite of 'withershins' or 'widdershins'. In a number of traditions it is considered lucky to travel deasil and unlucky to travel withershins. Going withershins around a church was considered to be particularly dangerous, leaving you vulnerable to supernatural powers.

decacuminated
adjective
having the top cut off

decubitus
noun
(medical) one's posture in bed

decumbiture
noun
the time when a sick person takes to bed

deglutition
noun
(physiology) the act or power of swallowing

dégringolade
noun
1 a sudden descent
2 a quick deterioration
verb
to make a rapid descent

dehisce
verb
to gape, burst open
> ஃThis word is used predominantly in medical and botanical contexts, where both wounds and pods can dehisce.

deipnosophist
noun
a person who converses learnedly at dinner, a table philosopher
> ஃThis impressive word is derived from *Deipnosophistai*, the title of a work by Athenaeus. It is a combination of Greek *deipnon* meaning 'dinner' and *sophos* meaning 'wise'. It is pronounced 'dip-*nos*-uh-fist', with the stress on the second syllable. Use it the next time you are having dinner with a friend.

delassation
noun
fatigue, weariness

deltiology
noun
the study and collection of picture postcards

dendrolatry
noun
the worship of trees

der-doing
adjective
doing daring deeds
> ஃThis adjective and the noun 'derring-do' came into being through

confusion over the Middle English *durran do*, which literally means 'daring to do'. It was misunderstood, and interpreted as meaning 'daring deeds'. The adjective 'der-doing' is construed to be an adjective meaning 'doing daring deeds'. However, as this confusion arose in the Elizabethan age, it is only fair to accept the meanings these words have been given.

desinent or desinential
adjective
(archaic) terminal

desudation
noun
1 a violent sweating
2 an eruption of small pimples

dewlap
noun
1 the pendulous skin under the throat of cattle, dogs, etc
2 the fleshy wattle of the turkey

diabology
noun
1 the doctrine of devils
2 the study of devils

diachoresis
noun
(medical) the act of excretion

diacle
noun
a small compass, especially one on a boat

dicacity
noun
raillery, banter
    ❧This archaic word comes from Latin *dicax* meaning 'sarcastic'. The related adjective is 'dicacious'.

dido

noun

1 an antic, a caper
2 a frivolous or mischievous act

> ટ≫The origin of this word is unknown but it is unconnected to the Dido of Virgil's *Aeneid* who committed suicide on being abandoned by Aeneas, an act which could in no way be described as frivolous or a caper.

digamy

noun

a second marriage (after the death of a partner or divorce)

dilaniate

verb

to tear into pieces

dimble

noun

(dialect) a dell, a dingle

dimpsy

noun

(South West England) twilight

dingle-dangle

adverb

swinging to and fro

adjective

swinging, dangling

> ટ≫This word is still enjoying life within the irritating children's action song 'Dingle-Dangle Scarecrow'.

dinnle

(Scots)

verb

to tingle, shake or vibrate, or cause to tingle, shake or vibrate

noun

a thrill, vibration, tremor or tingling

diphyodont
adjective
having two successive sets of teeth (milk and permanent)
noun
an animal with these
   ❧Most mammals, including humans, are diphyodonts.

dividivi
noun
1 the curved pods of a small tropical American tree (*Caesalpinia coriaria*), used for tanning and dyeing
2 the tree itself

dod
(Scots)
noun
a slight fit of ill-humour
plural noun
the dods the sulks
   ❧This comes from Gaelic *dod* meaning 'peevishness'.

doddymite
noun
(Essex) an infant

doddypoll
noun
(obsolete) a blockhead

dodman
noun
(dialect) a snail

dongle
noun
1 (computing) a device plugged into a computer to allow an authorised application to run
2 a device used in the illegal cloning of mobile phones

dottle
noun
a plug, especially of tobacco left at the bottom of a pipe

doughnutting
noun
the surrounding of a speaker in parliament by other members to give an impression, especially to television viewers, of a packed house

doula
noun
a woman whose job is to provide emotional and physical, but not medical, care to a woman in labour and to the parents and child after birth
> ટ▸The origin of this word could be off-putting to anyone considering it as a career: in Greek *doule* means 'a slave girl'.

doup
noun
(Scots)
1 the bottom section of an eggshell
2 the buttocks
3 the bottom or end of anything
> ટ▸This is pronounced 'dowp'.

doxographer
noun
a compiler of opinions of philosophers.

doxology
noun
(Christianity) a hymn or liturgical formula ascribing glory to God

drabbet
noun
a coarse linen fabric used for smock-frocks

draconites
noun
a precious stone fabled to come from a dragon's brain
> ⍤This mythical stone, pronounced 'drak-on-*ait*-eez' with the stress on the third syllable, was believed by alchemists to have magical powers that endowed the holder with invincibility. This, however, was only the case if the stone had been taken from a living dragon. A stone from a dead dragon was just a stone.

dreikanter
noun
a pebble faceted by windblown sand, properly having three faces

droog
noun
a gang-member, specifically a violent hooligan of the type portrayed by Anthony Burgess in his novel *A Clockwork Orange* (1962)
> ⍤Burgess himself coined this word, basing it upon Russian *drug* meaning 'a friend'.

droshky or drosky
noun
1 a low four-wheeled open carriage used in Russia
2 a German four-wheeled cab

drumble
verb
(dialect) to be sluggish

drumlin
noun
(geology) a usually oval ridge formed under the ice-sheet of the Glacial Period

duende
noun
(Spanish)
1 literally, a ghost, goblin, demon

2 inspiration, magnetism, ardour
    ❧The second meaning of 'duende' was first proposed by the Spanish playwright and poet Federico Garcia Lorca in a lecture ('Play and Theory of the Duende') in the 1930s. This inspiration is driven by the inevitability of death and the despair that knowledge brings.

dulcifluous
adjective
flowing sweetly

dulciloquy
noun
a soft manner of speaking

dumbledore
noun
(dialect) the bumblebee
    ❧This 18th-century word has received no little exposure in recent years since the author JK Rowling created the character of Albus Dumbledore, headmaster of the wizard school Hogwarts, in her Harry Potter novels.

dunch or dunsh
(Scots)
verb
1 to jog, nudge, bump
2 to butt
noun
a jog or push

dunderfunk or dandyfunk
noun
(nautical) a ship biscuit, soaked in water, mixed with fat and molasses, and baked in a pan
    ❧What a word!

duniewassal, dunniewassal or duniwassal
noun
a Highland gentleman of inferior rank

dupion
noun
1 a double cocoon, made by two silkworms spinning together
2 a kind of coarse silk made from these cocoons

durance
noun
(obsolete)
1 continuance
2 durability
3 a durable cloth
4 imprisonment

duvet day
noun
a day's absence which an employee is allowed to take at short notice when they can't face work but don't have the energy to pretend to be sick

dvandva
noun
(grammar) a compound word, each element being equal in status
→Some examples of dvandvas are 'tragicomedy' and 'bitter-sweet'. This is derived from Sanskrit *dvamdva* meaning 'a pair.

dysphoria
noun
1 impatience under affliction
2 morbid restlessness
3 uneasiness
4 absence of any feeling of wellbeing

dysteleology
noun
the study of functionless rudimentary organs in animals and plants

Ee

earworm
noun
a piece of music that, once heard, stays in your head for a long time no matter how hard you try to forget it

Ebionite
noun
a member of an early Jewish Christian sect, who believed they were bound by the law of Moses, who refuted the divinity of Jesus, and denied the apostleship of Paul
> This group was based in Jerusalem, and was reputedly led by James the Just, brother of Jesus.

ebriose
adjective
drunk
> There are dozens of words in English that mean 'drunk'. Most of them are slang. A sociologist might suggest that this is an indication of the importance of alcohol in British culture.

echinate or **echinated**
adjective
prickly like a hedgehog; bristly
> The pronunciation is '*ek*-in-ate' or '*ek*-in-ate-id', with the stress on the first syllable. In Greek *echinos* means 'a hedgehog'.

effluvium
noun
1 disagreeable vapours rising from decaying matter
2 minute particles that flow out from bodies
3 a generally unpleasant smell or exhalation

effodient
adjective
(zoology) habitually digging

eft
noun
1 a newt
2 (obsolete) a lizard
> ᔟ►This word is useful in explaining the linguistic phenomenon known as false splitting. The Old English word for the creature we now know as a newt was *efeta*. From this came the dialect versions *evet* and *eft*. The form *ewt* then developed, which would be preceded by the indefinite article 'an', to give 'an ewt'. Through the process of false splitting, the 'n' of 'an' became attached to the front of 'ewt' and it became 'a newt'. This process was responsible for a number of current English words, including *adder*, *apron*, *nickname* and *umpire*.

eglu
noun
a brand of plastic chicken coop designed for city gardens
> ᔟ►This word is a blend of 'egg' and 'igloo', making a punning reference to the shape of the coop itself.

ego-surfing
noun
the activity of searching for one's own name on the internet
> ᔟ►There can be few people with access to a computer who have not indulged in this activity, and compared their hit rate to that of their friends.

eidolon
noun
1 an image
2 a phantom or apparition
3 a confusing reflection or reflected image
4 an ideal or idealized person or thing

eleutheromania
noun
a manic desire for freedom

eleutherophobia
noun
a morbid or excessive fear of freedom

elf belt
noun
a belt believed to offer protection against elves
   ɜᴏThis item dates back as far as the 17th century in Orkney, where there are church archives reporting the destruction of such a belt by the local presbytery. That was not the end of the elf belt however. A search of the internet will show that this accessory is highly prized by groups of online gamers as a defence against evil spirits, trolls, etc.

elflocks
plural noun
locks of hair tangled together, supposedly by elves
   ɜᴏIn Shakespeare's *Romeo and Juliet*, Mercutio declares that Queen Mab 'bakes the elflocks in foul sluttish hairs'.

elide
verb
1 to cut off (especially a syllable in verse)
2 to suppress or abridge
   ɜᴏThe act or process of eliding is 'elision'.

embonpoint
adjective
stout, plump or full in figure
noun
stoutness, plumpness or well-fed condition

    👉This word comes from French *en bon point* meaning 'in good form'. In recent years a new noun usage has developed. When people talk about a woman's *embonpoint*, they are often referring to a well-developed bust, rather than a well-fed body.

emerods
plural noun
(Bible)
1 haemorrhoids
2 representations of them in gold, used as charms

    👉In the Bible, 1 Samuel chapter 5, verse 6 describes the affliction visited on the Philistines after they had taken the Ark of the Covenant: 'But the hand of the Lord was heavy upon them of Ashdod, and he destroyed them, and smote them with emerods'. This was a translation of the Hebrew *ophalim* which can also be translated as 'swellings' or 'tumours'. Scholars now believe that this affliction was most likely bubonic plague and the *ophalim* were its buboes. Such is the discomfort of haemorrhoids that for centuries it seemed reasonable that they would be considered due punishment for stealing the holiest relic in Judaism.

energumen
noun
a person who is possessed by a demon

ennui
noun
1 a feeling of weariness or languor
2 boredom

epeolatry
noun
the worship of words

    👉Clearly, some of us are practitioners of this worship

epergne
noun
a branched ornamental centrepiece for a table

epicanthus
noun
a fold of skin over the inner canthus of the eye, characteristic of the Mongolian race
> ❧Various members of my family had or have partial epicanthic folds, attributable no doubt to the fact that our grandmother, who came from the Shetland Islands, had forefathers who were operators or captains of tea clipper ships to China, and one of them brought back a little more than tea.

epicist
noun
one who writes an epic

epigon or epigone
noun
1 one of a later generation
2 a son or successor
3 an inferior follower or imitator

epopee
noun
1 epic poetry
2 an epic poem

Erdgeist
noun
an earth-spirit
> ❧In German folklore, an *Erdgeist* is a gnome.

ergophobia
noun
an abnormal dislike of work
> ❧It is up to the individual to decide whether their dislike of their work

is abnormal, therefore making them 'ergophobic', or normal, making them, well, normal.

erinaceous
adjective
of, relating to, or resembling a hedgehog

ersatz
noun
1 a substitute
2 (military) a supplementary reserve from which waste can be made good
adjective
1 substitute
2 fake

erythrophobia
noun
1 a fear of blushing
2 an aversion to the colour red
•*Erythros* is the Greek word for 'red'.

esclandre
noun
1 notoriety
2 any unpleasantness
•This French word has the same root as the English word 'scandal', which is Latin *scandalum*.

eske
plural noun
(Orkney) small spots of rain that precede a heavy storm

essorant
adjective
about to soar

estrangelo or estranghelo
noun
a cursive form of the old Syriac alphabet

estrapade
noun
a horse's attempt to throw its rider

euouae or evovae
noun
names for a cadence in Gregorian chant
ৼ This word was created by taking every second letter from 'seculorum Amen' (formerly written 'secvlorvm Amen'), a passage in the doxology 'Gloria Patri'. However, the most interesting fact about this word is that it is the longest in the English language to contain only vowels.

euripus
noun
1 an arm of the sea with strong currents, specifically that between Euboea and Boeotia in classical Greece
2 a ditch round the arena in a Roman amphitheatre

eutaxy
noun
good order

eutony
noun
a discipline that emphasizes the awareness and regulation of the body's muscular tone
ৼ This discipline was developed in the 20th century by the Danish teacher Gerda Alexander. The name combines Greek *eu* meaning 'well' and Latin *tonus* meaning 'tone'.

eutrapelia
noun
wit, ease and urbanity of conversation

exobiology

noun

the study of (possible) extraterrestrial life

>Possible or probable? With an estimated 100 billion stars in our galaxy, the Milky Way, and with another 100 billion stars in each of the 100 billion likely galaxies, what are the chances?

exsufflation

noun

1 expiration
2 forced expiration
3 exorcism by blowing

eyrar

noun

a group of swans

Ff

famble
noun
(slang) the hand

fanfaron
noun
1 a person who uses bravado
2 a blusterer or braggart

fankle
noun
(Scots) a tangle, a muddle

fantod
noun
a fidgety, fussy person, especially a ship's officer
plural noun
fantods fidgets; anxiety

> ஆThe origin of this peculiar word is obscure. The plural form is an American usage, commonly found as 'the howling fantods' or 'the screaming fantods'. It means the same as 'the heebie-jeebies'.

fantoosh
adjective
(Scots)

1 fashionable
2 pretentious or showy
    ☙This Scots word is possibly related to the English dialect word fanty-sheeny meaning 'fussy or showy', which is itself derived from Italian *fantoccino* meaning 'a marionette'.

femerall
noun
an outlet for smoke in a roof

fescue
noun
1 a type of grass
2 a pointer used in teaching

filemot
adjective
of a dead-leaf colour, dull brown
    ☙This comes from French *feuillemorte* meaning 'a dead leaf'.

filibuster
noun
1 a pirate or buccaneer
2 a military adventurer or revolutionary
3 (Parliament) a person who obstructs legislation by making lengthy speeches, introducing motions, etc
4 (Parliament) obstruction by such means in a legislative body
    ☙This is a good example of how a word meaning something exciting can end up meaning something deadly dull.

filipendulous
adjective
hanging by or strung on a thread

fimble
noun
the male plant of hemp
    ☙Curiously, this word is derived from Dutch *femel* meaning 'female'. It was used to describe the plant now classified by botanists as being

male. Parents of small children will also know that, in the alternative universe of children's television, a Fimble can also be a stripy furry creature with a talent for finding things.

fimblefamble
noun
a lie, a false excuse

finagle
verb
to obtain by guile or swindling
noun
an instance of finagling
> ➥This word comes from the English dialect *fainaigue* meaning 'to cheat or shirk'.

finical
adjective
affectedly or excessively precise in unimportant matters

fipple
noun
1 (dialect) the underlip
2 (in wind instruments) the plug in the mouthpiece, often together with the sharp edge against which it directs the wind
> ➥In Old Norse *flipi* means 'a horse's lip'.

fizgig
noun
1 a giddy or flirtatious girl
2 a firework of damp powder
3 a gimcrack, whimsy or trifle
4 a harpoon
5 (Australian slang) a police informer

flâneur
noun
a person who saunters about, a stroller

&❧From French *flâner* meaning 'to lounge', a flâneur is literally one who lounges or saunters about. However, the word has taken on further associations, so that it implies one who wanders about a city, recording his impressions and experiences – an urbane commentator upon the fashions and foibles of city life.

fleshling
noun
a sensualist

flew
noun
the pendulous upper lip of a bloodhound or similar dog

flexitarian
noun
a vegetarian who is less than strict about what they eat

flibbertigibbet
noun
1 a flighty, gossipy or mischievous person
2 an imp

&❧This word is known to millions across the world from the *Sound of Music* song 'How do you solve a problem like Maria?'
How do you find a word that means Maria?
A flibbertijibbet! A will-o'-the wisp! A clown!

flimp
verb
to rob (someone) while a partner hustles

flinterkin
noun
(Orkney) a dry cowpat

flipe
verb
to fold back, as a sleeve

floccinaucinihilipilification
noun
(facetious) setting at little or no value
> &❧This word is reputed to have been coined as a joke, and is frequently quoted as an example of an exceptionally long word in the English language. It combines various Latin words that indicate insignificance – *flocci* and *nauci* meaning 'at a trifle', *nihili* meaning 'at nothing' and *pili* meaning 'at a hair', with *facere* meaning 'to make'.

flother
noun
a snowflake
> &❧This word is so rare as to have been found only once in written English, in a 13th-century manuscript.

folderol or falderal
noun
1 a meaningless refrain in songs
2 any kind of flimsy trifle

footle
verb
to trifle, waste time or potter
noun
silly nonsense

foppotee or fopasty
noun
(obsolete) a simple-minded person

forswink
verb
(obsolete) to exhaust by labour
> &❧This word from Old English *for-* meaning 'utterly' and *swincan* meaning 'to labour' must surely merit a revival.

fossick

verb

(Australian)

1 to search for gold, on the surface or in abandoned workings
2 to rummage
3 to dig out

foudroyant

adjective

1 (archaic) thundering
2 (archaic) dazzling
3 (pathology) sudden and overwhelming

    ➤This is the present participle of the French *foudroyer* meaning 'to strike with lightning'. The noun *foudre* meaning 'lightning' is found in the phrase 'coup de foudre' which is love at first sight.

fouter

noun

a fig, as a type of worthlessness

verb

(Scots) to mess around aimlessly

frazil

noun

1 ground-ice
2 ice in small spikes and plates in rapid streams

freegan

noun

a person who eats the discarded food found in litter bins and thrown out from restaurants and supermarkets

freekeh

noun

an Arab dish made from a type of roasted green wheat

frowzy or frowsy
adjective
1 fusty
2 stuffy or offensive
3 unkempt

fubby or fubsy
adjective
(dialect) chubby; squat

fugacious
adjective
1 inclined to run away or flee
2 fleeting
3 (of petals, etc) readily shed
> Derived from Latin *fugere* meaning 'to flee', this word is related to 'fugitive'.

furbelow
noun
(archaic)
1 a plaited border or flounce
2 a superfluous ornament

furkid
noun
a domestic animal that is treated as if it is its owner's child
> There is a movement among some animal lovers to proscribe the use of 'pet', as it is considered to be demeaning to the animal. Preferred terms include 'companion animal' and 'furkid', the latter conferring on the animal a status equivalent to that of the owner's child. Some pets might consider this a demotion in status.

furze
noun
gorse

fuscous

adjective
1 brown
2 dingy

fushion

noun

(Scots) strength, vitality or essential virtue

→Remember this word. It will enable you to answer that great pub quiz question: 'Name three words that end in *–shion*'. The obvious ones are 'fashion' and 'cushion'.

fusioneer

noun

a person who is interested in and conducts experiments in nuclear fusion

fustilugs

noun

(obsolete) a gross overgrown person, especially a woman

Gg

galactometer
noun
an instrument for calculating the specific gravity of milk

galleass or galliass
noun
a vessel built like a galley, but larger and heavier

galligaskins
plural noun
1 wide hose or breeches worn in the 16th and 17th centuries
2 leggings

galliwasp
noun
a West Indian lizard

garbologist
noun
(US)
1 (facetious) a dustman, a rubbish-collector
2 a person who studies a society's waste materials in order to make deductions about the lifestyles of its people

gardyloo
interjection
the old warning cry in Edinburgh and other cities before throwing slops out of the window into the street
noun
the slops so thrown, or the act of throwing
> ☞This is apparently from the would-be French *gare de l'eau* for *gare l'eau*, meaning 'beware of the water', a euphemism for the contents of the chamber pots in question.

gasconism
noun
boastfulness
> ☞This comes from *Gascon* which, as well as meaning 'a person from Gascony', can mean 'a braggart or boaster'. Hence gasconism is boastfulness. We must assume that the natives of Gascony had a reputation in the 18th century for bragging, rather like Texans have in the US nowadays.

gastromancy
noun
1 divination by sounds from the belly, ie ventriloquism
2 divination by large-bellied glasses
> ☞Perhaps the government could use this as a new method of economic forecasting.

gawpus
noun
(dialect) a silly person

geggery
noun
(Scots) trickery

gemütlich
adjective
1 amiable
2 comfortable

3 cosy
> ০►This German adjective and its related noun *Gemütlichkeit* meaning 'kindness, comfort or cosiness' are just two of a number of words from that language that have been taken into English without alteration. Others include *Schadenfreude, Zeitgeist, wanderlust, realpolitik, angst, doppelganger* and *leitmotiv*.

genethliac
adjective
(obsolete) relating to a birthday or to the casting of horoscopes

gentoo
noun
1 a Falkland Island penguin
2 (obsolete) a speaker of Telugu, an Indian language
3 (archaic) a non-Christian from India, a Hindu
> ০►Derived from Portuguese *gentio* meaning 'a Gentile', it is unclear how the name came to apply to the penguin.

gerund-grinder
noun
a pedantic teacher

ginglymus
noun
a joint that permits movement in one plane only, a hinge joint
> ০►This word can be pronounced '*jing*-li-muhs' or '*ging*-li-muhs', with the stress on the first syllable.

girn or gurn
verb
(dialect)
1 to snarl
2 to grimace, make a grotesque face
3 to complain peevishly
> ০►There was a wonderful photograph in the press recently of gurning champion Tommy Mattinson, pulling his most ridiculous face in front of the Queen. Her reaction was a wonder to behold. I suspect her sense

of humour was lurking and she was fighting the desire to burst into a
winning gurn of her own.

glabrous
adjective
hairless, smooth

glaikit
adjective
(Scots)
foolish; stupid, daft

glamping
noun
a form of 'glamorous camping' that involves a top-of-the-range
designer tent, luxury equipment and fine food and wine

Glassite
noun
a follower of John *Glas* (1695-1773), who was deposed in 1728
from the ministry of the Church of Scotland for maintaining that
a congregation with its eldership is, in its discipline, subject to no
jurisdiction but that of Jesus Christ
   ⮞The Glassites were also known as Sandemanians, after John Glas's son-
      in-law Robert *Sandeman*, who developed much of the sect's doctrine.

glimmer-gowk
noun
(dialect) an owl

glister
verb
to sparkle, glitter
   ⮞This word appears in the correct version of one of the most misquoted
      lines in English literature: *The Merchant of Venice*, Act II, Scene vii:
         'All that glisters is not gold;
         Often have you heard that told'
      The correct version reads 'glisters' not 'glitters'.

globigerina
noun
1 a minute marine invertebrate of the genus *Globigerina*, with a shell of globe-shaped chambers in a spiral
2 a shell of this type

globish
noun
a simplified version of English spoken by many non-native speakers, comprising only the most basic words and phrases

globophobia
noun
a morbid fear of balloons

glurge
noun
a mawkishly sentimental story circulated by email, the accuracy of which is dubious

glyptic
adjective
relating to carving, especially gem-carving

gnathic
adjective
(in anatomy) relating to the jaws

gobe-mouches
noun
1 a flycatcher (bird)
2 an insectivorous plant
3 a credulous person

    {>This word comes from French *gober* meaning 'to swallow' and *mouche* meaning 'a fly'. The third sense presumably developed from the idea that a credulous person will listen to any old rubbish in open-mouthed belief.

goliard

noun

any of a band of medieval wandering students and scholars noted
for their riotous behaviour and especially their satirical Latin poems
lampooning the Church, most of which were credited to a mythical
Bishop Golias

goluptious

adjective

delicious, voluptuous

gongoozler

noun

(dialect) an idle observer, especially one who watches the activity on
a canal

    ❧Another probably uniquely British hobby. Do the Dutch do it?

gong-fermor

noun

(in the Middle Ages) a person who cleans out privies at night and
sells the waste as a fertilizer

    ❧*Gong* is another Middle English word for 'a privy', and *fermor* is a
    variant of 'farmer'. If this sounds repulsive or ridiculous, remember that
    these days there is a thriving trade in tiger dung from zoos, which, it is
    claimed, keeps domestic cats at bay.

gor-belly

noun

(obsolete)

1 a big belly

2 a big-bellied person

gordita

noun

(in Mexican cookery) a small thick corn tortilla typically filled with
chicken, vegetables, meat etc

grackle
noun
1 a myna or similar bird
2 an American blackbird of the family *Icteridae*

grammaticaster
noun
(archaic) someone who is concerned with the petty details of grammar

grampus
noun
1 technically, Risso's dolphin
2 a popular name for many whales, especially the killer
3 (archaic) someone who breathes heavily and loudly, a puffer and blower

graphomania
noun
an obsession with writing

greet
verb
(Scots) to weep
> ଛ⇒This Anglo-Saxon word has died out in standard English, which is a shame. Nothing quite encapsulates the essence of a miserable, moaning child as beautifully as the popular Scots phrase 'a greetin'-faced wean'. The last assembly of a local council before an election is the 'greeting meeting'.

gribble
noun
a small marine isopod that bores into timber under water

grille-peerer
noun
one of a group of clergymen in the 1940s who used to haunt the

stacks of the London Library to look up the skirts of women browsing above

&>I spotted a bookshop version of the grille-peerer in Foyles in the 1960s – his methods were slightly more advanced than his library-bound counterparts. He crouched low, appearing to study the books on a lower shelf close to a female browser, while conducting his real 'research' using a mirror on the end of a stick.

grockle
noun
(derogatory) a tourist or incomer, especially in SW England

growlery
noun
(archaic) a retreat for times of ill-humour

&>This is a marvellous word for a marvellous thing: 'Begone! I go to my growlery!'

guddle
(Scots)
verb
1 to fish with the hands by groping under the stones or banks of a stream
2 to dabble in, or play messily with, something liquid
noun
a mess, muddle, confusion

&>'Guddling for trout' is the same as standard English 'trout tickling'.

gue, gu or gju
noun
a kind of viol formerly played in Shetland

guga
noun
(Scots) a young gannet, eaten as a delicacy, especially in the Hebrides

gurgitator

noun

a person who takes part in competitive eating contests

> ट्ऀThe organization known as IFOCE (International Federation of Competitive Eating) runs eating events worldwide. Generally there is a time limit of about 15 minutes during which the gurgitators have to consume as many or as much of the chosen food as possible. The 2007 record for hot dog eating was 66 (with buns) in 12 minutes. Do you want mustard with that?

gushel

noun

(Orkney) a sudden prolonged gust of wind

gyromancy

noun

divination by walking in a circle and falling from giddiness

> ट्ऀThis must surely be the ultimate method of forecasting the fortunes of a British political party.

Hh

haboob

noun

a sandstorm

haecciety

noun

(in medieval philosophy) that element of existence on which
individuality depends, hereness-and-nowness

> ☙The medieval theologian and philosopher John Duns Scotus coined
> this word, basing it on Latin *haec* meaning 'this' and *–itas* 'denoting a
> state or quality'. It is pronounced 'hek-*see*-it-i', with the stress on the
> second syllable.

halsfang

noun

(in Anglo-Saxon England) a wooden frame, supported by an upright
pillar or post, with holes through which the head and hands were put
as a punishment; the pillory

hamadryad

noun

1 (in classical mythology) a wood nymph who died with the tree in
which she dwelt
2 the king cobra, a large poisonous snake
3 a large Ethiopian baboon

hamble
verb
1 to mutilate, make (a dog) useless for hunting (by cutting the balls of its feet)
2 (dialect) to limp, to stumble

hapax legomenon
noun
a word or phrase that is found once only
 ↓This Greek phrase literally means 'said only once'.

hedonics
noun
that part of ethics or of psychology that deals with pleasure

Heimweh
noun
(German) home-sickness

helminth
noun
a worm

hen-hussy
noun
a man who meddles with women's affairs

hepaticocholangiocholecystenterostomy
noun
a surgical procedure in which the gall bladder is linked to the hepatic duct and to the intestine

hermeticist
noun
someone who is a follower of or believer in the philosophy ascribed to Hermes Trismegistus

Hesperus or Hesper
noun
Venus as the evening star

heuch or heugh
noun
(Scots)
1 a crag
2 a ravine or steep-sided valley
3 a quarry-face
4 an excavation, especially for coal

high-muck-a-muck
noun
(North American) an important, pompous person
> ?This word sounds marvellously insulting. It comes from Chinook Jargon *hiu* meaning 'plenty' and *muckamuck* meaning 'food'.

himbo
noun
(slang) a man who is attractive but dull and unintelligent; a male bimbo

hippophagy
noun
feeding on horseflesh

hippopotomonstrosesquipedaliophobia
noun
a fear of long words
> ?Words that are *sesquipedalian* are long or polysyllabic. *Phobia* is of course a fear or dislike. *Hippopoto-* and *monstro-* are pseudo-prefixes which are added to emphasize the scale of these long words and in the process, as a little joke, to make the word itself something a sufferer would fear. Finding this word did kind of worry me.

hircine
adjective
1 goat-like
2 having a strong goatish smell

hirple
(Scots)
verb
to walk or run as if lame
noun
a limping gait
> ۞This one is useful to remember when asked for a word that rhymes with 'purple'.

hirsel
(Scots)
noun
1 a stock of sheep
2 a multitude
3 the ground occupied by a hirsel of sheep
verb
to put in different groups
> ۞This word is derived from Old Norse *hirzla* meaning 'safekeeping', which itself comes from *hirtha* meaning 'to herd'. The former Prime Minister Sir Alec Douglas-Home became Lord Home of the Hirsel when he received his life peerage in 1974, the Hirsel being the family home in Berwickshire, taking its name from the third noun sense.

hobbledehoy or hobberdehoy
noun
an awkward youth, neither man nor boy
> ۞As well as appearing in the writings of Jonathan Swift and Anthony Trollope, 'hobbledehoy' can be found in the nursery rhyme with actions 'This is the Way the Ladies Ride'. The ladies ride 'tri, tre, tre, tree', the gentlemen ride 'gallop-a-trot', while the farmers ride 'hobbledehoy'.

Hobson-Jobson
noun
1 festal excitement, especially at the Muharram ceremonies in Islam
2 the modification of names and words introduced from foreign languages, which the popular ear assimilates to already familiar sound, as in the case of the word Hobson-Jobson itself

→The Arabic lament *Ya Hasan, ya Hosain!* meaning 'Oh Hasan, oh Hosain!' is part of the ritual of the Mourning of Muharram in Islam, which commemorates the death of Husayn ibn Ali, Muhammad's grandson, at the Battle of Karbala. British soldiers in India, on hearing this cry, changed its unfamiliar sound into something that made more sense to them: Hobson-Jobson. In 1886 *Hobson-Jobson*, a dictionary of well-known Anglo-Indian words and phrases by Arthur C Burnell and Sir Henry Yule was published, popularizing the word further.

hodmandod or hodmedod
noun
(dialect) a snail

hoker
noun
scorn or derision
verb
to scorn, to mock

homilophobia
noun
an abnormal fear of sermons

hoplology
noun
the study of weapons

hopple
verb
to restrain by tying the feet together
noun
a fetter for horses, etc when left to graze

horripilation

noun

a contraction of the cutaneous muscles causing erection of the hairs and gooseflesh

> ❧This word comes from Latin *horrere* meaning 'to bristle' and *pilus* meaning ' a hair', and is therefore connected to 'horrendous', 'horrible', 'horrid' and 'horrify'.

horrisonant

adjective

dreadful-sounding

horse-godmother

noun

(dialect) a fat clumsy woman

hortus siccus

noun

a collection of dried plants, a herbarium

> ❧This is Latin for 'dried garden'.

houri

noun

1 a nymph of the Muslim paradise

2 a voluptuously alluring woman

> ❧The origin of this is Persian *huri*, itself from Arabic *huriya* meaning 'a black-eyed girl'. This makes an interesting cultural contrast to Western ideals of beauty, which are generally focused on those with blue eyes, so much so that the phrase 'blue-eyed boy' means 'a favourite who can do no wrong'.

howdah or houdah

noun

a seat fixed on an elephant's back

howlet

noun

(Scots)

1 an owlet
2 an owl

hoyden
noun
a tomboy

humdudgeon
noun
1 (Scots) an unnecessary outcry
2 (dialect) low spirits

humgruffin
noun
a terrible person

hwyl
noun
(Welsh)
1 divine inspiration in oratory
2 emotional fervour

hyperbole
noun
a rhetorical figure which produces a vivid impression by extravagant
and obvious exaggeration

hyperborean
adjective
belonging to the extreme north
noun
an inhabitant of the extreme north
> The ancient Greeks believed that there was a race of people – the
> *Hyperboreoi* – who lived in sunshine beyond the Boreas, the north
> wind.

hypocorism or hypocorisma
noun
a pet-name; a diminutive or abbreviated name

hypsography
noun
1 the branch of geography dealing with the measurement and mapping of heights above sea level
2 a map showing topographic relief
3 a method of making such a map

Ii

iceblink
noun
a glare in the sky caused by light reflected from distant masses of ice

ichthyolatry
noun
the worship of fish

iddy-umpty
noun
(military slang) Morse code
> ⚘This apparently dates from the time of the Raj, from nicknames used to teach Morse code to Indian troops. A dot was 'iddy' and a dash was 'umpty', so letter P (dot dash dash dot) was 'iddy umpty umpty iddy'.

idioglossia
noun
1 a condition in which pronunciation is so bad as to be quite unintelligible
2 a private language developed between two or more children, especially twins
> ⚘This literally means 'private language' as it comes from Greek *idios* meaning 'own' and *glossa* meaning 'tongue or language'.

idioticon

noun
a vocabulary of a particular dialect or district

ignis fatuus

noun
1 the light produced by combustion of marsh-gas, which may lead a traveller into danger; will-o'-the-wisp
2 any delusive ideal or hope that may lead one astray

immortelle

noun
1 an everlasting flower
2 a china replica of flowers, as a graveyard monument

imposex

noun
the superimposition of male sexual characteristics onto female gastropods, caused by certain pollutants

imprimatur

noun
a licence or permission to print a book, etc
ઠ⊶This Latin word is translated literally as 'let it be printed'.

incirclet

noun
a small circle or spiral

incompossible

adjective
incapable of coexisting

incony *or* inconie

adjective
fine, delicate, pretty
ઠ⊶Act IV of Shakespeare's *Love's Labours Lost* contains the following line:
'O' my troth, most sweet jests! most incony vulgar wit!'

indigent
adjective
1 impoverished
2 in need, especially of means of subsistence

ingluvies
noun
the crop or craw of birds

injelly
verb
to place as if in jelly
> In his poem 'Audley Court', Tennyson describes the food offered at a picnic, including the following, which seems to be a kind of game pie:
>> a pasty costly-made,
>> Where quail and pigeon, lark and leveret lay,
>> Like fossils of the rock, with golden yolks
>> Imbedded and injellied.

insolation
noun
1 exposure to the sun's rays
2 solar radiation falling upon a given surface

insufflation
noun
1 the act of breathing on anything, especially in baptism or exorcism
2 the act of blowing air, power, etc into a cavity or on a surface
3 the act of blowing gas or a medication in powder form into a body cavity

interfenestration
noun
the spacing of windows

interlard
verb
1 to mix in, as fat with lean

2 to intersperse (one's speech or writing) with unusual words

interlunation
noun
the dark time between the old moon and the new

interrobang
noun
a punctuation mark consisting of a question mark superimposed on an exclamation mark
> ❧ This rare punctuation mark is used in questions that themselves imply astonishment or horror, such as: '*What* did you pay for that house‽'

intrepidation
noun
fearlessness, bravery

invaletudinary
adjective
sickly or infirm
> ❧ At first sight it would appear that this word would mean the opposite of 'valetudinary', but it does in fact mean the same, that is 'sickly'. As is the case with 'flammable' and 'inflammable', the prefix 'in-' does not always indicate negation.

invection
noun
a severe accusation or denunciation

inveigle
verb
1 to entice
2 to persuade by cajolery
3 to wheedle

ipsedixitism
noun
the practice of making dogmatic pronouncements

ॐ*Ipse dixit*, a Latin phrase meaning literally 'he himself said it', is a dogmatic statement or dictum.

isabel, isabella or isabelline

noun
a dingy yellowish grey colour
adjective
of this colour

ॐThe origin of this is unclear. It has been suggested that it relates to Isabella, daughter of Philip II of Spain, who did not change her linen for three years until Ostend was taken, but this is impossible as the word predates the siege of Ostend. A similar legend is ascribed to Isabella of Castile, and this would have been chronologically possible, but the connection has not been proved.

isinglass

noun
1 a material, mainly gelatine, obtained from sturgeons' air-bladders and other sources
2 thin transparent sheets of mica

izzat

noun
1 public esteem
2 honour, reputation, prestige

ॐThis Urdu word, from Arabic *'izzah* meaning 'glory', is an important concept in Islam.

Jj

Japhetic

adjective

1 of European race

2 relating to a number of European and near-Eastern non-Indo-European languages formerly thought to be related and to belong to some pre-Indo-European grouping

>According to the Old Testament, Japheth was one of Noah's three sons, the others being Ham and Shem. After the flood each son went to a different land to settle, and these three men between them were responsible for populating the earth, and creating its three races: the Japhetic, the Hamitic and the Semitic. Japheth went to 'the isles of the Gentiles', commonly believed to be the isles of Greece, and hence the Japhetic race became the European race.

Jehoiada-box

noun

a child's savings-bank

>In 2 Kings chapter 12 verse 9 of the Old Testament there is the story of the priest Jehoiada and his plan to collect money for the repair of the temple: 'But Jehoiada the priest took a chest, and bored a hole in the lid of it, and set it beside the altar, on the right side as one cometh into the house of the Lord'.

jeistiecor

noun

(Scots)

a close-fitting garment

> ঽ◈This obsolete term is derived from French *juste au corps* meaning 'close-fitting to the body'.

jellygraph

noun

a former device for copying that used a plate of jelly

> ঽ◈Office life is much the poorer for the demise of this device.

jippi-jappa

noun

a palm-like tree of tropical America, the fibre from whose leaves is used for panama hats

> ঽ◈This takes its name from *Jipijapa*, a city in western Ecuador famed for the production of panama hats.

jobble

verb

to move jerkily like a sea running in irregular waves.

jobernowl

noun

a stupid person

> ঽ◈The word is apparently derived from the French *jobard*, meaning 'a noodle' and the English nowl, meaning 'the top of the head'.

jocko

noun

a chimpanzee

> ঽ◈The word came into use via French, from the West African *ncheko*.

jogger's paw

noun

inflammation of a dog's paw caused by its owner dragging it along while jogging

jougs
noun

(in Scottish history) an instrument of punishment consisting of an iron collar attached to a wall or post and put round an offender's neck

ক⋗The word is probably derived from Old French *joug*, 'a yoke', from Latin *jugum*.

juglandaceous
adjective

of or pertaining to the walnut genus of trees

ক⋗The word is derived from Latin *jūglāns*, from *Jovis glāns* 'Jove's acorn'.

jumart
noun

the supposed offspring of a bull and a mare, or a stallion and a cow

ক⋗The word is derived from French.

Kk

kalotypography
noun
the art of printing in a beautiful manner
  ❧The word is derived from Greek *kallos* 'beauty'.

kark
verb
(Australian slang) to break down, or to die

katzenjammer
noun
1 (in North America) a hangover or similar state of emotional distress
2 an uproar or clamour
  ❧The word is derived from a German term meaning, literally, 'cats' misery'.

kavass
noun
an armed servant in Turkey
  ❧The word is derived from the Arabic *qawwās*

keckle
verb
to protect something, such as a cable, by binding it with rope, etc

keelivine or keelyvine

noun
(Scots) a lead pencil

kef, kaif or kif

noun
1 a state of dreamy repose
2 a drug, such as marijuana, smoked to produce such a state
> ≥»The word is derived from the Arabic *kaif* 'pleasure'. It is pronounced 'kayf'.

keister

noun
1 (in American slang) the buttocks; arse
2 a safe or strong-box
3 a case or box
> ≥»The word is probably derived from the German *kiste* 'chest, case'. This is supported by the fact that it is pronounced '*kee*-ster'.

kengestion

noun
a type of traffic congestion peculiar to London
> ≥»While former London mayor Ken Livingstone's congestion charge undoubtedly has its fans, many commentators have noted irritating phenomena which seem to have served only to increase the capital's traffic chaos. Notable features of 'kengestion' include traffic lights which seem to be red for between one and two minutes and then green for between six and ten seconds; bendy buses which when they are not catching fire or dragging cyclists to their deaths can be observed in stationary jams whilst carrying negligible numbers of passengers; and random multiple roadworks where no workers are to be seen.

kennebunker

noun
a big suitcase

kexy
adjective
dried-up and wilting
> The word is derived from kex meaning dried stems of various plants.

kibitzer
noun
(North American slang) an onlooker (at cards, etc) who gives
unwanted advice; an interferer
> The word is derived from Yiddish.

kickie-wickie
noun
a wife
> The word is found in Shakespeare.

kilfud-yoking
noun
(Scots) a fireside disputation
> The word is derived from *kilfuddie* 'the aperture for feeding a kiln' and
> *yoking* 'joining together'.

killcrop
noun
a greedy, insatiable baby; a changeling
> The word is derived from German.

kindergarchy
noun
tyranny of or rule by children.
> A new word coined by, amongst others, Joseph Epstein in an article in
> *The Weekly Standard*, on how we have become dominated by children
> and all their needs and demands, and are obsessed with how to bring
> them up, making them the centre of all attention. A possible alternative
> might be 'kinderachy'.

kine

noun
cows

kinin

noun
1 a plant hormone that promotes cell division and is used commercially as a preservative for cut flowers
2 any of a group of polypeptides in the blood, causing dilation of the blood vessels and contraction of smooth muscles
ₑ➤The word is derived from Greek *kīn(ēsis)* 'movement'.

kinkajou

noun
a South American tree-dwelling animal related to the raccoon
ₑ➤The word is apparently derived from a Native American term misapplied.

kinnikinick *or* killikinick

noun
1 a mixture used by Native Americans as a substitute for tobacco
2 a species of cornel or other plant forming part of the mixture

knick-knackatory

noun
a collection of knick-knacks
ₑ➤This is a super word which brings to mind the collections of ornamental (or would-be ornamental) objects lovingly assembled and proudly displayed by so many young girls.

knobber

noun
a stag in its second year

knurling

noun
mouldings or other woodwork elaborated into a series of knobs

kobold
noun
a spirit of the mines; a benevolent creature who may secretly help with domestic work
> The word is derived from German and is the origin of the name of the metal element cobalt.

kreng
noun
the carcass of a whale after the blubber has been removed
> The word is derived from Dutch.

kromesky
noun
a croquette wrapped in bacon or calf's udder, and fried
> The word is derived from Polish *kroméczka* meaning 'little slice'.

kumiss
noun
fermented mares' milk
> The word is derived from Russian *kumis*, from Tatar *kumiz*.

kvetch
verb
to complain or whine, especially incessantly
> The word is derived from Yiddish.

Ll

lablab
noun
a tropical bean (*Dolichos lablab*) with edible pods
෧ The word is derived from Arabic.

lagniappe
noun
something given beyond what is strictly required; a gratuity
෧ The word is ultimately derived from Quechua, via American Spanish and Louisiana French. It is pronounced 'lahn-*yap*' with the stress on the second syllable.

laldie
noun
(Scots) a beating or thrashing (as punishment); vigorous action of any kind
෧ The word is perhaps connected with Old English *læl*, meaning a whip, weal or bruise.

lallygag
verb
(US informal)
1 to idle or loiter
2 to caress, especially publicly

lambdacism

noun

1 a too frequent use of words containing *l*-sounds
2 faulty pronunciation of the sound of *l*
3 a defective pronunciation of *r*, making it sound like *l*
➤The word is derived from the Greek name for the letter *lambda*, corresponding to the Roman *l*.

lambent

adjective

1 moving about as if touching lightly like a flame; gliding or playing over
2 flickering; softly radiant, glowing
3 (especially of wit) light and brilliant
➤The word is derived from the Latin *lambere* 'to lick'.

lamia

noun

in Greek and Roman mythology, a bloodsucking serpent-witch
➤The word is pronounced '*lay*-me-ah', with the stress on the first syllable.

lanuginose

adjective

downy; covered with fine soft hair
➤The word is derived from the Latin *lānūgō* meaning 'down'.

lectual

adjective

especially of a disease, confining to the bed
➤The word is derived from the Latin *lectus* meaning 'bed'.

left-facedness

noun

the theory that the left side of the face is more expressive than the right

leiotrichous
adjective
straight-haired
> The word is derived from the Greek *leios* meaning 'smooth' and *thrix, trichos* meaning 'hair'. The word is pronounced 'lie-*aw*-trik-uss' with the stress on the second syllable.

lemniscate
noun
the mathematical symbol (∞) which represents infinity
> The word is derived from the Latin *lēmniscātus* meaning 'ribboned', from the Greek *lēmniskos* meaning 'ribbon'. The word is pronounced 'lem-*niss*-kate' with the stress on the second syllable.

leucipotomy or leucippotomy
noun
the art or practice of cutting of figures in chalk uplands
> I found this word in a guidebook to the chalk hill figures of Wiltshire while staying in a house there in 2007

level-coil
noun
an old Christmas game in which the players changed seats
> This is derived from the French *lever le cul* meaning 'to lift the buttocks'.

lickerish
adjective
1 dainty or tempting
2 eager to taste or enjoy
3 lecherous
> The word is a variant form of lecherous.

lilly-pilly
noun
an Australian tree of the myrtle family

limn
verb
to draw or paint, especially in watercolours; originally to illuminate
with ornamental letters, etc.
> ☙The word derives from Old French luminer or enluminer, from Latin
> *lūmināre* or *illūmināre*, meaning 'to cast light upon'. The 'n' is silent.

limosis
noun
an abnormally ravenous appetite
> ☙The origin of the word is the Greek *līmos*, meaning 'hunger'.

linsey-woolsey
noun
1 a thin coarse material of linen and wool mixed, or inferior wool with
cotton
2 (in Shakespeare) gibberish
adjective
1 made of linen and wool
2 neither one thing nor another; presenting a confusing mixture

liripipe or liripoop
noun
1 the long tail of a graduate's hood
2 a part or lesson committed to memory
3 a silly person
> ☙This obsolete word derives from a Late Latin term whose origin is
> unknown.

lissom
adjective
lithe, nimble, flexible
> ☙This is a form of lithesome.

litholatry
noun
the worship of stones

lithotripter

noun

a device that crushes stones in the bladder, etc by ultrasound

> ৯►The '-tripter' element of the word drives from the Greek *thryptika*, meaning 'breakers of stones'.

Lob-lie-by-the-fire

noun

(folklore) a benevolent creature who may secretly help with domestic work at night in return for a bowl of cream

> ৯►The Lob-lie-by-the-fire is otherwise known as the 'lubber fiend', probably best known from Milton's *L'Allegro*

loblolly

noun

1 a name for various American pine trees
2 (dialect) thick gruel, hence ship's medicine
3 (dialect) a lout
4 (US) a muddy swamp or mire

loblolly boy

noun

the attendant of a ship's surgeon

locavore

noun

a person who will eat only locally-produced food

locofoco

noun

1 (US) a match for striking, a friction match
2 one of the extreme section of the Democratic Party of 1835, known as the Equal Rights Party

logizomechanophobia

noun

an abnormal fear of computers

logodaedalus
noun

someone skilled in the manipulative use of words

    This is Latinized form of Greek *logodaidaolos*, from *logos* meaning 'a word' and *Daidalos*, 'Daedalus'. Daedalus was the character in Greek mythology who created the Cretan labyrinth where the Minotaur was kept, and who made the wings with which he and his son Icarus fled Crete. He was a skilled craftsman and inventor (the name Daedalus itself means 'cunning worker'). Hence, a person who has as much skill with words is a 'logodaedalus'.

logogriph
noun

a riddle in which a word is to be found from other words made up of its letters, or from synonyms of these

    The word is derived from Greek *logos*, meaning 'word' and *grīphos*, 'net, riddle'.

logophile
noun

a lover of words

logorrhoea
noun

excessive flow of words, uncontrollable garrulity

    From Greek *logos*, meaning 'word' and *rhoia*, 'flow'.

lollapalooza
noun

(US slang) something excellent or wonderful

    This particularly euphonic word is also spelled lollapalootza or lalapaloosa

lollygag
verb

1 (in North America) to idle or loiter
2 to caress, especially in public

lophiodon
noun
an extinct mammal related to the tapir

loppened
adjective
(Orkney) numbed by the cold
> Like many Orkney terms, this has a Scandinavian origin, in this case it derives from Norwegian dialect *loppen*, meaning 'numb'.

Lorelei
noun
(in German legend) a siren of the Rhine who lured sailors to their death
> From the German *Lurlei*, the name of the rock she was believed to inhabit.

luciferin
noun
a protein-like substance in the luminous organs of certain animals, especially glow-worms and fireflies
> The word is derived from Latin *lucifer*, meaning 'light-bringer'.

luckenbooth
noun
a booth or shop, especially of the type found in Edinburgh in the 18th century
> In Scots, the adjective 'lucken' means 'closed'. Still common today are luckenbooth brooches, the silver heart-shaped brooches originally sold from such booths

Lucy Stoner
noun
(US) a woman who keeps her maiden name after marriage
> The original Lucy Stone (1818-93) was an American suffragist.

lugubrious
adjective
1 mournful
2 dismal

lummox
noun
(informal) a stupid, clumsy person

lunitidal
adjective
relating to the moon and its influence on the tide

lutraphobia
noun
an abnormal fear of otters

luz
noun
a bone supposed by Rabbinical writers to be indestructible, probably the sacrum

Mm

macarism

noun

a beatitude

> ৯৯The word is derived from Greek *makar*, meaning 'happy'.

madefy

verb

to moisten or make wet

> ৯৯This archaic term derives from Latin *madefacere*, from *madēre*, meaning 'to be wet'.

maduro

noun

a dark, strong type of cigar

> ৯৯The word is essentially a Spanish term meaning 'mature'.

maelid

noun

an apple nymph

> ৯৯The word is derived from Greek *mēlon*, meaning 'apple'.

maieutic

adjective

(of the Socratic method of inquiry) bringing out latent thoughts and ideas

&This word comes from Greek *maieutikos*, from *maia* meaning 'a good woman, a midwife'. Socrates, whose mother was a midwife, referred to himself as 'a midwife to men's thoughts'.

malacophilous
noun
(of a plant) pollinated by snails
&From Greek *malakos*, meaning 'soft' and *phileein*, to love.

malapropism
noun
the misapplication of words without mispronunciation, or an example of this, such as 'He is the very pineapple of politeness' (for pinnacle) or 'She's as headstrong as an allegory on the banks of the Nile' (for alligator).
&The famous eponym of this characteristic is Mrs Malaprop in Sheridan's play *The Rivals* (1775), who uses words malapropos.

Malebolge
noun
1 the eighth circle of Dante's Hell
2 (in figurative use) a place characterized by filth or iniquity
&From Italian *male bolge*, meaning 'bad holes or pits'.

maledicent
adjective
cursing
&The word is derived from Latin *maledīcere*, from male, meaning 'ill' and *dīcere* 'to speak'.

mallemaroking
noun
the carousing of seamen in icebound ships
&This rare, especially in the 21st century, word is derived from Dutch *mallemerok*, meaning 'a romping woman'.

mamelon
noun
a rounded hill or protuberance in a landscape
ခ►Essentially, this is a French word meaning 'nipple'.

mandrolic
adjective
performed manually in a time-consuming way rather than automatically or computationally

mani
noun
a stone prayer wall in a Tibetan Buddhist temple, usually carved with sacred images or texts
ခ►This word is derived from Tibetan, from Sanskrit *mañi*, meaning 'precious stone'.

Manichee
noun
a believer in Manicheanism, the belief that everything springs from two chief principles, light and darkness, or good and evil

manitou
noun
a spirit or sacred object among certain Native American tribes
ခ►The word is derived from an Algonquin term.

mansard
noun
(in architecture) a four-sided roof, each side being in two parts, the lower part sloping more steeply than the upper
ခ►The word is derived from French *mansarde*, after the 17th-century French architect François Mansart.

marchpane
noun
another word for marzipan, used until the 19th century

marsupium

noun

(zoology) the pouch of a marsupial animal

martinet

noun

a strict disciplinarian

→The original Martinet was a French general in the reign of Louis XIV, who drew up a severe system of drills for new recruits.

maudlinism

noun

the tearful stage of drunkenness

→The word is formed from the adjective *maudlin*, which in turn derives from Middle English *Maudelein*, through Old French and Latin, from Greek *Magdalēnē*, (woman) of Magdala, from the assumption that Mary Magdalene was the penitent woman referred to in the Bible, Luke chapter 7, verse 38.

mawk

noun

a dialect word for a maggot

→The word is derived from Old Norse *mathkr*, meaning 'maggot'.

meacock

adjective

timorous, effeminate, cowardly

noun

a timorous, effeminate or cowardly person, a milksop

megrim

noun

1 vertigo or dizziness
2 (in archaic and Scottish use) a whim, a caprice
3 an obsolete form of the word migraine
4 (especially in North America) the plural form **megrims** means depression or doldrums

melomania
noun
a craze for music
> ❧The word is derived from the Greek *melos*, meaning 'song' and *maniā*, meaning 'madness'.

merdivorous
adjective
(of an insect) dung-eating
> ❧The word is derived from Latin *merda*, meaning 'dung' and *vorāre*, 'to devour'.

meretricious
adjective
1 (Originally) of the nature of or relating to prostitution or characteristic of a prostitute
2 superficially attractive but of no real value or merit
3 flashy; gaudy; insincere
> ❧The original meaning of this word can be seen in its etymology, which is Latin *meretrix* meaning 'a prostitute'.

merrythought
noun
an obsolete term for the wishbone of a bird

metromania
noun
a mania for writing verse
> ❧The word is derived from Old French *metre*, ultimately from the Greek *metron*, meaning 'measurement', and *maniā*, meaning 'madness'.

Milquetoast
noun
a very timid, unassertive person
> ❧The American cartoonist HT Webster created a character of this name and disposition in a 1920s comic strip.

milsey
noun
a Scots term for a milk-strainer
> The word is derived from milk, and either *sye* or *sile*, both of which mean 'a strainer'.

mim
adjective
(Scots and dialect) demure, prim
> The word probably evolved through imitation of a primly closed mouth.

mimsy
adjective
prim, demure or prudish
> The word is obviously related to mim (above), but may have been influenced by Lewis Carroll's invented word, as in 'All mimsy were the borogroves' in his nonsense poem 'Jabberwocky'.

misocainea
noun
a hatred of new things or new ideas

misocapnic
adjective
hating smoke, especially that of tobacco
> Both elements of this word derive from Greek, where *mīseein* means 'to hate' and *kapnos* means 'smoke'.

misqueme
verb
to offend or displease someone

mizmaze
noun
1 a labyrinth
2 bewilderment

mizuna
noun
a Japanese vegetable of the cabbage family that grows in large rosettes of feathery leaves

mizzen
noun
in a three-masted vessel, the hindmost of the fore-and-aft sails
   ‽The word is derived from the French *misaine*, meaning 'foresail, foremast', from Italian *mezzana* 'mizzensail', from Late Latin *mediānus* middle, from Latin *medius* middle; the development of meaning is puzzling

mizzle
noun
fine rain
   ‽This word is probably related to the Late German *miseln*, meaning 'mist'.

mobisode
noun
a short film or episode from a longer piece intended for watching on a mobile phone or digital media player

moirologist
noun
someone paid to mourn at a funeral, especially ostentatiously

molinet
noun
a stick used to whip drinking chocolate in the 18th century
   ‽This word derives from the French *moulinet*, meaning 'little mill'.

momic
noun
a female comedian whose material mostly springs from the experience of motherhood

momzer or mamzer
noun
1 (Judaism) an illegitimate child, the child of an unrecognized marriage
2 (US slang) a detestable or untrustworthy person
꜕Like many of the most descriptive US words, this is from Yiddish.

mondegreen
noun
a phrase, often humorous or nonsensical, that results from mishearing the lyrics of a song
꜕The term was coined in 1954 by American writer Sylvia Wright after she had mistaken the phrase (from the traditional Scots ballad 'The Bonny Earl of Moray') 'laid him on the green' for 'Lady Mondegreen'.

monology
noun
the habit of monopolizing a conversation, turning it into a monologue

monophthong
noun
a simple vowel sound
꜕This word derives from Greek *monophthongos*, from *monos*, meaning 'single, alone', and *phthongos*, meaning 'sound, vowel'.

monticule
noun
a hill, mound or other little elevation
꜕This word derives from Latin *monticulus*, a diminutive form of *mōns*, meaning 'mountain'.

moon-glade
noun
the track of moonlight on water

morganatic
adjective
relating to a marriage between people of unequal rank (latterly only

where one is of a reigning house), the marriage being valid, the children legitimate but unable to inherit the higher rank, and the lower-born spouse not being granted the other's title.

&This word, at once charmingly antique and businesslike, derives from Late Latin *morganātica*, a gift from a bridegroom to his bride.

morkin
noun
an animal that has died by accident

&This word derives from Anglo-French *mortekine*, ultimately from Latin *mors*, meaning 'death'.

moronolexicophobia
noun
a fear of daft dictionaries

&Who could suffer from this? That's just silly.

moslings
noun
the thin shavings taken off by the currier in dressing skins

moudiewart
noun
a Scots term for a mouldwarp, that is, a mole (the animal)

&This is a word based on describing what the creature does. In Old English *molde* means 'mould' or 'earth', and *weorpan* is 'to throw'.

mubble-fubbles
noun
a state of low spirits

muckluck
noun
an Inuit sealskin boot

mugwump
noun
1 a Native American chief

2 a person of great importance, or one who thinks himself or herself to be so
3 someone who keeps politically aloof
   ҿ❧The first, and oldest, sense is the original meaning of the word, derived from Algonquian *mugquomp*, meaning 'great chief'.

mulligrubs
noun
1 colic
2 sulkiness

mumpsimus
noun
1 a view or opinion stubbornly held, even when shown to be misguided
2 a person holding such a view, or one adhering stubbornly to old ways
   ҿ❧Mumpsimus relates to an old story about a priest who, for many years, had been using the wrong word in mass. He had been saying 'mumpsimus' for 'sumpsimus', which means 'we have received'. On having this error pointed out to him he refused to change it, preferring to stick with his familiar, although incorrect and meaningless, 'mumpsimus'.

mungo
noun
the waste produced in a woollen mill from hard spun or felted cloth, or from tearing up old clothes, used in making cheap cloth

murine
adjective
1 mouselike
2 belonging to the mouse family or subfamily

murklins
adverb
in darkness

muster
noun
a collective name for a group of peacocks

mutchkin
noun
an obsolete Scottish liquid measure, three-quarters of an imperial pint, or a quarter of an old Scottish pint
 ह•Like several Scots words, this is derived from Dutch, in this case the term *mudseken*.

mutton-thumper
noun
a clumsy bookbinder
 ह•Presumably, the mutton is a reference to the sheepskin used in bookbinding.

myomancy
noun
divination by observing the way in which mice move when released from a cage
 ह•This word is derived from Greek *mys*, meaning 'mouse' and *manteiā*, meaning 'divination'.

mythomania
noun
(in psychiatry) lying or exaggerating to an abnormal extent
 ह•This word is derived from Greek *mythos*, meaning 'myth, story, or talk' and *maniā*, meaning 'madness'.

Nn

nacket
noun
a snack, light lunch

nacre
noun
mother-of-pearl or a shellfish yielding it

nannick
verb
(Essex) to fidget

napiform
adjective
turnip-shaped
    ›This word derives from *nāpus* the Latin for 'turnip'.

narcolepsy
noun
a pathological condition marked by short attacks of irresistible drowsiness
    ›A sufferer from this condition is called a narcoleptic.

nasutus
noun
(entomology) a genus or species of termite that has a soldier caste characterized by a pronounced 'nose' or proboscis

natiform
adjective
buttock-shaped

nattier blue
noun
a soft azure
   ࢩ➤This colour is named after the French painter JM Nattier (1685-1786).

necromantic
adjective
of or relating to necromancy, the art of revealing future events by calling up and interrogating the spirits of the dead

neogamist
noun
a person recently married

nepenthe
noun
a drink or drug causing sorrow to be forgotten
   ࢩ➤The word is pronounced 'ni-*pen*-thee', with the stress on the second syllable; its origin is a Greek term meaning 'not grief' which first appears in Homer's Odyssey. It is also the name of a very strong, richly seductive Sardinian red wine made from local 'Cannonau' grapes. Cannonau was a favourite of the Italian poet Gabriele D'Annunzio, who was the first to liken this wine to Homer's mythical potion. Nepenthe is also a type of insectivorous plant, the pitcher plant, which lures its prey into deep slippery pitchers containing syrupy liquid.

nephalism
noun
total abstinence from alcoholic drinks

neophilia
noun
a love of novelty and new things

> ઠ•Dr. Thomas Stuttaford, who writes in the *The Times*, wrote an amusing and interesting article about this concept. Dr. Richard Ebstein of the Herzog Hospital in Jerusalem and Dr Robert Cloninger of the Washington School of Medicine in St Louis believe that the constant desire for change, and to change, is a trait of many personality disorders, but it is related to a particular dopamine receptor gene (D4DR). Dr Stuttaford explained that in his opinion, our former prime minister Tony Blair suffered from this disorder, which we should now perhaps call Ebstein-Cloninger Syndrome.

neuston
noun
minute organisms that float or swim on the surface of water

neutercane
noun
a tropical storm that has not yet been given a name

nicky-tam
noun
(Scots) a piece of string, etc worn below the knee to keep the bottom of the trouser-leg lifted clear in dirty work or to exclude dust, etc

nidor
noun
a strong smell or fume, especially of animal substances cooking or burning

niminy-piminy
adjective
affectedly fine or delicate
noun
affected delicacy

> ઠ•This happens to be one of the longest words that can be typed with the right hand only.

nipcheese
noun
a stingy person

niplet
noun
a small nipple
> This word seems to have been a particular favourite of the 17th-century English poet Robert Herrick, as in his poem 'How Lillies Came White':
>> He with his pretty finger prest
>> The rubie niplet of her breast.

nipperty-tipperty
adjective
(Scots) finical or mincing

nomic
adjective
1 pertaining to a discoverable law in science or logic, ie a law whose validity is not dependent on specified conditions
2 pertaining to the musical and literary genre of nomes

nong
noun
(Australia and New Zealand) a slang term for fool, idiot

noop
noun
the orange-red sweet-flavoured fruit of the cloudberry, a low plant of North America and Northern Europe, related to the bramble, and usually found on high open moorland

nopster
noun
a woman who works at raising the nap on cloth

nostopathy
noun
an abnormal fear of going back to familiar places

nostos
noun
a Greek word for a poem describing a return or a return journey

notaphily
noun
the collecting of bank notes, cheques, etc as a hobby
»A hobby that I confess to having.

nubia
noun
a fleecy head-wrap formerly worn by women

nuciform
adjective
nut-shaped

nudibranchiate
adjective
of or belonging to members of the *Nudibranchia*, shell-less marine gastropods with external, often branched gills on the back and the sides of the body

nullipara
noun
a woman who has never given birth to a child

numen
noun
a presiding deity

numerotage
noun
the numbering of yarns so as to denote their fineness

numpty
noun
(Scots) an idiot

nystagmus
noun
a spasmodic involuntary lateral oscillatory movement of the eyes

Oo

Oblomovism
noun
the inability to bring oneself to act, lazy inertia
> ໒The novel *Oblomov* by Russian author Ivan Goncharov, published in 1859, featured an eponymous hero who was the embodiment of physical and mental laziness.

obumbrate
verb
to overshadow
> ໒The word is pronounced 'oh-*bum*-brait', with the stress on the second syllable.

ocarina
noun
a fluty-toned wind instrument, originally made of terracotta, egg-shaped, with a long mouthpiece
> ໒This word derives from Italian, a diminutive of *oca*, meaning 'a goose'.

occiput
noun
the back of the head or skull

ochlocracy
noun
mob rule

oculolinctus
noun
sexual arousal from licking one's partner's eyeball

oeillade
noun
an ogle, glance or wink
> ᕲThe word is derived from French *oeil*, meaning 'eye'.

oggie or oggy
noun
a slang term used in Cornwall for a pasty

oggin
noun
a sailors' slang term for the sea
> ᕲThe word is said to be from earlier *hogwash*, meaning 'the sea'.

olecranon
noun
a projection at the upper end of the ulna, at the elbow

olisbos
noun
a dildo

olykoek
noun
(US) a kind of doughnut
> ᕲPronounced '*ol*-ee-cook', this word is derived from Dutch *oliekoek*, meaning 'oil-cake'.

omnibology
noun
the hobby of watching and photographing buses
> ᕲAnother of these curious fetishes. Peculiar, it would seem, to the British male. Do men in France, Italy, Russia or even the United States indulge in such hobbies?

omoplatoscopy
noun
divination by observing the cracks in a burning shoulder-blade

omphalomancy
noun
divination of the number of future children from the knots in the umbilical cord

omphaloskepsis
noun
the act of navel-gazing

oneirocritic
noun
an interpreter of dreams

oneirataxia
noun
the inability to differentiate between dreams and reality

oneirology
noun
the study of dreams

onychocryptosis
noun
the condition of having an ingrowing toenail

onychomancy
noun
divination by studying the fingernails

onychophagist
noun
someone who bites their fingernails

ooidal
adjective
egg-shaped

oology
noun
the science of study of birds' eggs

oose
noun
(Scots) fluff, particularly of the kind that collects under beds.
ξ►The word is pronounced 'ooss'.

operculum
noun
1 (botany) a cover or lid
2 (zoology) the plate over the entrance of a shell
3 the gill-cover of fishes
4 a coal-hole cover in a pavement
5 (facetious) a hat
ξ►The word is derived from Latin, from *operāre*, meaning 'to cover'.

ophthalmophobia
noun
the fear of being stared at

opine
verb
to suppose; to form or express as an opinion

oporice
noun
a former medicine prepared from quinces, pomegranates, etc
ξ►Pronounced 'oh-*por*-iss-ee', with the stress on the second syllable,
this word is derived from Greek *opōrikē*, from *opōrā*, meaning 'late
summer, summer fruits'.

opportunivore

noun

a person who will eat anything they can find, including discarded food

opsimathy

noun

learning obtained late in life

> ꙮThe word is derived from the Greek *opse*, meaning 'late' and *mathē*, meaning 'learning'.

oriflamme

noun

a small banner of red silk split into several points, carried on a gilt staff, the ancient royal standard of France

> ꙮThe word is derived from Late Latin *auriflamma*, meaning 'golden flame'.

orrery

noun

a clockwork model of the solar system

> ꙮThe device was named after Charles Boyle, fourth Earl of Orrery (1676-1731), for whom one was made.

otolith

noun

a calcareous concretion in the ear of various animals, the movement of which helps the animal to maintain equilibrium

oud

noun

an Arab stringed instrument resembling a lute or mandolin

oundy

adjective

an obsolete word meaning 'wavy'

ouroboros
noun
(in mythology) a representation of a serpent with its tail in its mouth, symbolizing completion, totality, endlessness, etc

outernet
noun
a word coined to represent all of the traditional media (such as print, television and film) that are not part of the Internet

outfangthief
noun
(history) the right of judging and fining thieves pursued and brought back from outside one's own jurisdiction

outligger
noun
(on a vessel) a projecting spar for extending a sail

ouvreuse
noun
a cinema usherette in France, originally a woman employed to open theatre boxes for patrons
   ❧Somehow this word seems to conjure up a much more exotic image than our own 'usherette'.

ovicide
noun
the killing of sheep

ovulite
noun
a fossil egg

oxter
noun
(Scots, Irish and Northern English) the armpit

verb
to take under one's arm; to support someone by taking their arm
  ~The Old English word for armpit is *oxta*.

ozaena
noun
a fetid discharge from the nostrils

ozokerite or ozocerite
noun
a waxy natural paraffin

Pp

paillette
noun
a spangle
> ❧This originally French word is pronounced 'pal-*yet*' with stress on the second syllable.

paletot
noun
a loose overcoat
> ❧The word is pronounced '*pal*-toe', with stress on the first syllable.

palilalia
noun
a speech abnormality characterized by the increasingly rapid repetition of words or phrases

palingenesis
noun
(geology) the re-melting of rock followed by solidification in a different form

palinure
noun
a pilot or helmsman
> ❧In Virgil's *Aeneid*, Palinurus was helmsman of Aeneas' ship.

pandemonium
noun
a collective name for a group of parrots

pandiculation
noun
the act of stretching and yawning

paneity
noun
the state of being bread

Panglossian
adjective
taking an over-cheerful and optimistic view of the world as did Dr Pangloss in Voltaire's *Candide* (1759)

panidrosis
noun
a perspiration of the whole body

panjandrum
noun
a figure of great power and self-importance, a burlesque potentate
   This enormously self-important word is from the *Grand Panjandrum* in a string of nonsense made up by Samuel Foote (1720-77), English wit, actor and dramatist.

pannage
noun
1 food picked up by swine in the woods, mast
2 the right to pasture swine in a forest

pantagamy
noun
a word that ought to mean universal bachelorhood, applied with unconscious irony to the universal marriage of the 19th-century

American sect, the Perfectionists, in which every man in the community is the husband of every woman
  ﻬThe word is derived from the Greek *gamos*, meaning 'marriage' and *agamiā*, meaning 'bachelorhood'.

pantheism
noun
1 the doctrine that nature and the physical universe are interchangeable with God
2 belief in many or all gods

pantisocracy
noun
a community (planned in the 18th century by Coleridge and Southey) in which all should have equal power

pantle
noun
a snare used to catch birds

pantler
noun
a historical term for the officer in a great family who had charge of the bread and other provisions

pantogogue
noun
a medicine once believed capable of purging away all morbid humours
  ﻬThis word derives from Greek *pan*, meaning 'all', and *agōgos*, meaning 'leading'.

pantophobia
noun
1 morbid fear of everything
2 (by confusion with panophobia) causeless fear

papain
noun
a digestive enzyme in the juice of the pawpaw

papaphobia
noun
(facetious) a morbid fear of popes

parabolanus
noun
(in the early Eastern Church) a layman who tended the sick

paraguesia
noun
a perverted sense of taste

paraleipsis
noun
a rhetorical figure by which one fixes attention on a subject by pretending to neglect it
> Some examples of paraleipsis are 'I will not speak of his generosity' and 'I do a lot of work for charity but I don't like to talk about it'.

paraph
noun
a mark or flourish under one's signature
verb
1 to append a paraph to
2 to sign something with one's initials

paraphilia
noun
sexual perversion

paraskevidekatriaphobia
noun
a morbid fear of Friday the 13th
> This word is derived from the Greek *paraskevi*, meaning 'Friday', and *dekatria*, meaning 'thirteen'.

paroccipital
adjective
(anatomy) near the occiput

parrhesia
noun
boldness of speech

parvanimity
noun
smallness of mind

pasilaly
noun
a language that can be spoken by all

patibulary
adjective
of or relating to a gibbet or gallows

patristic
adjective
relating to the fathers of the Christian Church

paxwax
noun
the strong tendon in an animal's neck

pectoriloquy
noun
the sound of a patient's voice heard through the stethoscope when applied to the chest

pedantocracy
noun
government by pedants

pelf
noun
a derogatory word used to refer to money or riches
༆This word is derived from Old French *pelfre*, meaning 'booty'.

pelology
noun
the study of mud

pendragon
noun
an ancient British supreme chief
༆The word is derived from the Welsh *pen*, meaning 'head' and *dragon*, 'dragon' or 'dragon-standard'.

pentheraphobia
noun
an abnormal fear of one's mother-in-law

penult
noun
the last but one (ie penultimate) syllable

penumbra
noun
1 a partial or lighter shadow round the perfect or darker shadow produced by an eclipse or by a large unfocused light source shining on an opaque object
2 the less dark border of a sunspot
3 the part of a picture where the light and shade blend into each other

perruquier
noun
a wig-maker

petcock
noun
a small tap or valve for draining condensed steam from steam-engine cylinders, or for testing the water level in a boiler

pettifogging
adjective
paltry, trivial, or cavilling

pettitoes
noun
pigs' feet, when used as food

phaeic
adjective
dusky

phantasmagoria
noun
a fantastic dreamlike series of illusive images or of real forms
> ह This was the name given to a show of optical illusions in 1802 and it comes from French *phantasmagorie*, which itself is from Greek *phantasma* meaning 'an appearance' and perhaps *agora* meaning 'an assembly'.

phillumeny
noun
the collecting of matchbox labels
> ह The word is derived from Latin *lūmen*, meaning 'light'.

philopena
noun
1 a game in which each of two people eats a twin kernel of a nut, and one pays a forfeit to the other on certain conditions
2 the nut itself
3 the gift made as a forfeit
> ह The word is apparently derived from the German formula of claiming the gift, *Guten Morgen, Vielliebchen*, meaning 'Good morning, well-

beloved', confused with the Greek *philos*, meaning 'friend', and *poinā*, penalty, and with the German *Philippchen*, meaning 'little'.

philoxenia
noun
hospitality
> This originally Greek word is derived from *philos*, 'lover' and *xenos*, meaning 'guest, stranger'.

philtrum
noun
the hollow that runs from the base of the nose to the upper lip

phit
noun
the sound of a bullet being fired

phrontistery
noun
a thinking-place
> The word is derived from the Greek *phrontistērion*, applied by Aristophanes to the school of Socrates.

pibroch
noun
the classical music of the bagpipe, free in rhythm and consisting of theme and variations
> There are people who would insist that the bagpipe is incapable of producing any music at all (such as those in Shakespeare who, on hearing it, 'cannot contain their urine'). However, no art form is without both critics and enthusiasts.

pica
noun
an unnatural craving for unsuitable food
> This word is derived from *Pica*, the genus name for the omnivorous magpie. Many pregnant women experience this type of craving, the substances of their desire varying from coal and toothpaste to matches

and face cream. It would seem that the condition is, if anything, becoming more common.

picaroon
noun
a person who lives by his or her wits; a cheat; a pirate
> ⮬The literary term 'picaresque' is derived from this word, which itself comes from the Spanish *picarón*, meaning 'rogue'.

piggin
noun
a small pail or bowl constructed of staves and hoops, like a barrel

pigsney
noun
an archaic or dialect term of endearment (sometimes contempt), especially to a woman

pilgarlick
noun
1 (obsolete) a bald head, or a man sporting one
2 a poor wretch
3 in whimsical self-pity, oneself
> ⮬This is so called because of the subject of the first meaning's alleged resemblance to a peeled head of garlic.

pilliwinks
noun
an instrument of torture for crushing the fingers
> ⮬The origin of this word is unknown, but to modern ears it sounds more like a children's game than a cruel device.

pilose
adjective
hairy, especially when the hair is fairly soft

pinchbeck
noun
a yellow alloy of copper with much less zinc than ordinary brass,
simulating gold
    ➤The alloy was invented by Christopher Pinchbeck (c.1670-1732), an
       English watchmaker.

pinchpin
noun
a prostitute

pingo
noun
a large cone-shaped mound having a core of ice formed by the
upward expansion of freezing water surrounded by permafrost

pinguitude
noun
the state of being fat
    ➤The word is derived from the Latin *pinguis*, meaning 'fat'.

pixilated
adjective
bemused, bewildered; slightly crazy; intoxicated
    ➤This word is derived from 'pixie', meaning 'a small fairy', with the
       possible influence of 'titillated'. It should not be confused with the
       much more recent term pixellated, meaning 'made up of pixels'.

pizzle
noun
1 the penis
2 the penis of a bull used as an instrument of punishment, in flogging

placophobia
noun
a morbid fear of tombstones

planiloquent
adjective
talking in a direct manner, straight-talking

plinian eruption
noun
a type of volcanic eruption characterized by repeated explosions
   🙋Named after the Roman scholar and statesman Pliny the Elder, who observed the eruption of Vesuvius in AD 79 that destroyed Pompeii and cost him his life.

plouter
(Scots)
verb
to dabble in liquid, or to potter
noun
a paddling or dabbling

plumelet
noun
a little feather or tuft

plumulate
adjective
downy

pneumatology
noun
1 the theory of the existence of spirits or spiritual beings
2 (archaic) psychology
   🙋The word is derived from the Greek *pneuma, -atos*, meaning 'breath', from *pneein*, meaning 'to breathe'.

pneumonoultramicroscopicsilicovolcanoconiosis
noun
an artificial long name denoting a form of pneumoconiosis caused by very fine silicate or quartz dust

&This mouthful is believed to be the longest English word recorded in major dictionaries.

pobblebonk
noun
a popular name for *Limnodynastes dumerilli*, the Australian Eastern Banjo Frog
&The frog takes its proper name from its call being compared to the plunking of a banjo, and 'pobblebonk' is also an attempt to imitate this sound in words.

pocillovy
noun
the hobby of collecting egg cups
&This highly specialized word is derived from Latin *pocillum*, meaning 'a small cup'.

poger
noun
a passive, older male homosexual

pogonion
noun
the most prominent part of the chin
&The word is derived from the Greek *pōgōn*, meaning 'beard'.

pointillism or pointillisme
noun
(in painting) the use of separate dots of pure colour instead of mixed pigments

pollywog, polliwog, pollywog or polliwig
noun
a tadpole
&This delightful old word is derived from Middle English *pollwyggle*, meaning essentially 'head wiggle'.

polymicrian
adjective
condensing a lot into a small space

polyphloesboean
adjective
loud-roaring
> ईUSually, but not exclusively, used as an epithet of the sea, this word is derived from the Greek *polyphloisbos*, from *phloisbos*, meaning 'din'.

ponerology
noun
(theology) the doctrine of wickedness

pong
verb
(theatre slang) to make impromptu additions to one's part in order to extend it, to gag

popjoy
verb
to amuse oneself

popliteal
adjective
of the back of the knee

popple
verb
1 to flow tumblingly
2 to heave choppily
3 to bob up and down
4 to make the sound of rippling or bubbling

pornocracy
noun
the influence of courtesans, especially over the papal court in the earlier half of the 10th century

pot-valiant or pot-valorous
adjective
full of drink-inspired courage

prankle
verb
to prance lightly

premorse
adjective
ending abruptly, as if bitten off
  ᠁The word is derived from the Latin *praemorsus*, meaning 'bitten in
   front', from *prae* in front, and *mordāre*, *morsum* to bite

preterist
noun
(theology) someone who believes that the prophecies of the
Apocalypse have already been fulfilled

prick-me-dainty
(Scots)
adjective
over-precise
noun
an affected person

probang
noun
a slender flexible rod, tipped with a sponge or button, for passing
down the throat and into the oesophagus, in order to apply
medication or remove an obstruction
  ᠁The instrument was invented in the 17th century by the Welsh judge,
   Walter Rumsey, who called it a 'provang', but the word seems to have
   been influenced later by 'probe'.

proclivity
noun
an inclination or propensity

Procrustean
adjective
taking violent measures to ensure conformity to a standard
> ࣟFrom Procrustes, a legendary Greek robber, who stretched or cut his captives' legs to make them fit a bed. Putting an end to these capers was one of the hero Theseus' more public-spirited feats.

procuratrix
noun
the person in a nunnery who is responsible for practical matters

profundal
adjective
of or relating to the zone in an ocean or lake that lies below the level where light can penetrate

progymnasma
noun
a preliminary exercise in a discipline, especially rhetoric

proseology
noun
dull and confusing prose

prosody
noun
1 the study of the art of composing verse
2 the study of rhythm, stress and intonation in speech

prosopography
noun
1 a biographical sketch, a description of a person's appearance, character, life, etc
2 the compiling or study of such material

protalus rampart
noun
(geology) a mound or ridge formed when scree from a cliff gathers at the edge of a glacier or permanent snow patch

Protean
adjective
1 readily assuming different shapes
2 variable; inconstant
3 versatile
   ᕙ The word is derived from Proteus, an ancient Greek sea god who assumed many shapes to evade having to foretell the future.

protimesis
noun
(rhetoric) the enumeration of things according to their importance

proxemics
noun
the study of the human use of physical space in non-verbal communication, especially the distances that people maintain between themselves and others while interacting

prunt
noun
a moulded glass ornament attached to a glass object such as a vase

psephology
noun
the sociological and statistical study of election results and trends
   ᕙ The word is derived from *psēphos*, a Greek word for 'pebble', because pebbles were used in ancient Greece to cast votes.

psithurism
noun
a whispering sound, such as that of wind among leaves

psychalgia
noun
psychological pain or suffering

psychrophilic
adjective
(of plants) growing best at low temperatures

pteronophobia
noun
a morbid fear of being tickled by feathers
    ह≫Who doesn't have this phobia?

puddlies
noun
(Orkney) the bare feet

pudibund
adjective
shamefaced or prudish

puftaloon
noun
(in Australia) a type of fried cake, usually eaten hot with jam, honey or sugar (also known as pufftaloonas, puftaloonies, etc)

puggle
verb
(Scots) to reduce a person to a state of mental or physical exhaustion

puku
noun
an antelope found in southern central Africa, especially in swampy areas and near rivers

pulchritude
noun
beauty

&⤙The rather unlovely word is derived from the Latin *pulchritādō*, from *pulcher*, meaning 'beautiful'.

pumpkineer
noun
someone who cultivates giant pumpkins, especially with a view to entering them in competitions

pumple-nose
noun
an old term for a shaddock, especially a grapefruit
&⤙The word is a variation of 'pompelmoose', which came to English from the Dutch *pompelmoes*.

purdonium
noun
a kind of coal scuttle introduced in the 19th century by a Mr Purdon

purfle
verb
to ornament the edge of something, for example with embroidery or inlay
noun
1 a decorated border
2 a profile

purfled or purfly
adjective
short-winded

pygal
adjective
belonging to the rump or posteriors of an animal
noun
the posterior median plate of the carapace of tortoises
&⤙The word is derived from the Greek *pygē*, meaning 'rump'. It also forms the basis of the delightful words 'callipygian' an 'dasypygal'; words which readers of *Foyle's Philavery* will already be familiar with.

pyknic
adjective
(of a human physical type) characterized by short squat stature, small hands and feet, relatively short limbs, domed abdomen, short neck, and round face

> ཞ Pronounced in the same way as the alfresco meal, the word is derived from the Greek *pyknos*, meaning 'thick'. There is no connection between this word and the more familiar 'picnic'. 'Pyknic' is from Greek *pyknos* meaning 'thick' and 'picnic' comes from French *pique-nique*.

Pyrrhic victory
noun
a victory gained at too great a cost

> ཞ An allusion to an exclamation by Pyrrhus, ancient king of Epirus, after his defeat of the Romans at Heraclea on the Siris (280 BC), 'Another such victory and we are lost.'

pyx or pix
noun
1 a box
2 (RC Church) a vessel in which the host is kept after consecration, now usually that in which the host is carried to the sick
3 a box at the Royal Mint in which sample coins are kept for testing

qanat
noun
an underground tunnel for carrying irrigation water
> ❧Pronounced 'kah-*nat*' with the stress on the second syllable, this is
> essentially an Arabic word meaning 'pipe'.

qiviut
noun
the wool of the undercoat of the arctic musk ox

quackle
verb
(dialect) to quack

quadragenarian
noun
a person who is forty years old, or between forty and fifty

quahog
noun
an edible clam (*Venus mercenaria*) of the North American Atlantic
coast
> ❧This word derives from the Narraganset (a Native American language)
> *poquauhock*, and it is pronounced '*kwaw*-hog', with the stress on the
> first syllable

quakebuttock
noun
a cowardly person

quant
noun
a punting or jumping pole

quantophrenia
noun
an over-reliance on mathematical results and statistics, especially in fields where they may not be useful or relevant

quaquaversal
adjective
facing or bending all ways
    ӋThe word is derived from the Latin *quāquā*, meaning 'whithersoever' and *vertere*, meaning 'to turn'.

quarl
noun
a jellyfish

Quasimodo
noun
the first Sunday after Easter, Low Sunday
    ӋTraditionally in the Roman Catholic Church the opening part of the mass on this day is from 1 Peter chapter 2 verse 2: 'Quasi modo geniti infantes' meaning 'as new-born babies'. The Hunchback of Notre Dame, the central character of Victor Hugo's novel, is called Quasimodo because he was found outside abandoned outside Notre Dame on a Quasimodo Sunday.

quatrain
noun
(in poetry) a stanza of four lines, usually rhyming alternately

quean or quine
noun
1 an archaic word for a saucy girl or a woman of worthless character
2 (Scots) a girl
 ॐThe word is derived from Old English, and in north-east Scotland queyn or quine and the diminutives queynie or quinie are the ordinary words for a girl.

quetsch
noun
a variety of plum, or brandy distilled from it
 ॐThe word is derived from a German dialect term for a wild plum.

quiddle
verb ·
(dialect) to trifle

quink-goose
noun
the brent goose

quinnat
noun
the king salmon, a large salmon of the Pacific
 ॐThe word is derived from a Native American name.

quinquagenarian
noun
a person who is fifty years old, or between fifty and sixty
adjective
fifty years of age, or between fifty and sixty years of age

quinsy
noun
suppurative tonsillitis, acute inflammation of the tonsil with the formation of pus around it
 ॐThe word is derived from Late Latin *quinancia*, ultimately from the Greek *kyōn* meaning 'dog', and *anchein* meaning 'to throttle'.

quipu
noun
a mnemonic device consisting of various colours of knotted cords, used by the ancient Incas

quisling
noun
a person who aids the enemy, especially a native puppet prime minister set up by an occupying foreign power
> In World War II, Vidkun Quisling was Norwegian prime minister during the German occupation (1940-45) and was executed for high treason after the war.

quonk
noun
any accidental noise made too close to a microphone and thus disrupting a radio or television programme
verb
to make such a noise
> This word is imitative of an unexplained, unwelcome sound.

quotidian
adjective
1 daily; recurring daily
2 commonplace, everyday

Rr

rakehell
noun
an utterly debauched person
adjective
debauched

Ralph
noun
the imp of mischief in a printing house

ramfeezle
verb
(Scots) to weary out

ramollescence
noun
the act or process of softening, mollifying

rasophore
noun
a Greek Orthodox monk of the lowest grade

rassasy
verb
to satisfy (a person's hunger for food)

rastaquouère
noun
1 a social climber from the Mediterranean area or South America
2 a foreigner who is attractive but untrustworthy

rebus
noun
an enigmatical representation of a word or name by pictures representing the component parts of the word, as in a puzzle or a coat of arms; such a puzzle
> ই This word, deriving from Latin *rēs*, meaning 'thing', was given wider currency when the writer Ian Rankin chose it as the name of his detective hero in the best-selling 'Inspector Rebus' series of novels.

recidivism
noun
the habit of relapsing into crime

red biddy
noun
a drink made of red wine and methylated spirit
> ই The 'biddy' element in this expression probably derives from 'Biddy', a familiar form of the woman's name Bridget.

retromingent
adjective
(of an animal) urinating backwards
noun
love of anything, especially material objects, from, connected with or evoking the past
> ই Animals one should be wary of standing behind include camels, lions and raccoons.

rhedarious
adjective
of or relating to a carriage or chariot with four wheels

rhinotillexomania
noun
an abnormal and obsessive desire to pick one's nose
    🍂The word is derived from the Greek *rhino*, meaning 'nose' and *tillexis*, meaning 'habit of picking',

rhombicosidodecahedron
noun
a solid figure with 62 faces (20 triangles, 30 squares and 12 pentagons)

rhopalic
adjective
(of a verse) having each word a syllable longer than the one before

ribibe
noun
an obsolete word for an old crone

rictus
noun
1 (zoology) the gape, especially of a bird
2 unnatural gaping of the mouth, especially in horror

riga
noun
a loose-fitting robe worn by men in West Africa

rigescent
adjective
growing stiff, becoming rigid

riggite
noun
someone who likes to poke fun at others

ringxiety
noun
the mistaken but persistent belief that one's mobile phone is ringing

rockel
noun
a woman's cloak

rog
verb
an old word meaning to shake someone or something

romanesco
noun
a vegetable of the Brassica family with spiral rosettes that exhibit fractal geometry
  ❧This word derives from the Italian *broccolo romanesco*, meaning 'Romanesque broccoli'.

rookery
noun
1 a breeding-place of rooks in a group of trees
2 a breeding-place of penguins, seals, etc
3 a crowded cluster of slum tenements

rootle
verb
to grub, to rummage

roric
adjective
dewy
  ❧This word is derived from the Latin *rās* or *rāris*, meaning 'dew'.

rorqual
noun
any whale of the genus *Balaenoptera* (finback)

༐This word came into English via French, from Norwegian, ultimately from an Old Norse term meaning 'red whale'.

rosacea
noun
(medical) a chronic disease of the skin of the nose, cheeks and forehead, characterized by flushing and redness of the skin, pimples and pustules

roscid
adjective
dewy
༐Like roric, this word is derived from the Latin *rās* or *rāris*, meaning 'dew'.

rounceval
noun
1 (obsolete) a giant
2 (obsolete) a large, boisterous woman
3 a marrowfat pea
adjective
(obsolete) gigantic
༐It has been suggested that this might come from the town of Roncesvalles in the Pyrenees.

rous
adverb
suddenly, and with an impact

rowlyrag
noun
a type of volcanic stone quarried in the West Midlands, and often used for surfacing roads

roytish
adjective
an obsolete word meaning 'wild or irregular'.

rubefy
verb
to redden

rumbledethumps
noun
a Scottish dish of mashed potatoes with butter and seasoning, sometimes mixed with cabbage or turnip

rumgumption
noun
(Scots) common sense

rumpty-dooler
noun
a New Zealand slang word meaning something exceptionally good or fine of its type

Ss

sabbat

noun
a witches' midnight meeting

salebrous

adjective
rugged or rough
   ዽ>This word is derived from the Latin *salebra*, meaning 'rough road'.

salep

noun
a food or drug prepared from dried orchid tubers

saltation

noun
1 a leaping or jumping
2 (biology) an abrupt variation or mutation
3 (geology) the movement of a particle being transported by wind or water, resembling a series of leaps

sarn

noun
an obsolete word for pavement

scads
plural noun
(US) a large amount, a lot (especially of money)

scapulimancy
noun
divination by means of the cracks appearing in a burning shoulder blade

scavilones
noun
a type of underwear worn beneath their hose by men in the 16th century

scolion or skolion
noun
a short drinking song of ancient Greece, taken up by the guests in irregular succession

scomfish
verb
to stifle; to disgust

scripophily
noun
the collecting of bond and share certificates as a hobby, especially those of historical, etc interest

scrobicule
noun
(biology) a small pit or depression, as around the tubercles of a sea urchin

scroddled
adjective
(of pottery) made of clay straps of different colours

scuddick

noun

(dialect) something that is small in size or importance

scurriour or scurrier

noun

(obsolete) a scout

scuttlebutt

noun

(US) rumour or gossip

›In the days of sailing ships, a scuttlebutt was a cask with a hole cut in it for drinking water on board ship, and as such would be the ideal place to exchange gossip.

sebastomania

noun

religious mania

selenography

noun

mapping of the moon; the study of the moon's physical features

›The word is derived from the Greek *selene*, meaning 'moon'.

senescence

noun

the process of growing old, especially the physical changes such as the slowing down of metabolism and the breakdown of tissues that are characteristic of this process

serendipity

noun

the faculty of making fortunate or beneficial discoveries by accident

›The word was coined in 1754 by Horace Walpole from the title of the fairy tale *The Three Princes of Serendip* (Serendip being a former name for Sri Lanka), whose heroes 'were always making discoveries, by accidents and sagacity, of things they were not in quest of'.

serried
adjective
close-set; packed or grouped together without gaps

sesquipadality
noun
the tendency to use long or cumbersome words

sesquipedalian
adjective
1 tending to use long or cumbersome words
2 (of words) long, pedantic or polysyllabic
> ☙This word is derived from the Latin *sesquipedalia verba*, meaning 'words a foot and a half long', coined in Horace's *Ars Poetica*.

sesquipedaliophobia
noun
a fear of long words
> ☙See also *hippopotomonstrosesquipedaliophobia*.

shankum
noun
(Orkney) a person or animal whose legs are long and skinny

shebeen
noun
1 an illicit liquor shop
2 (in Ireland) illicit, usually home-made, alcohol
> ☙The word is derived from an Anglo-Irish term meaning 'little mug'.

shemozzle, shimozzle, shlemozzle or schemozzle
noun
1 a mess
2 a scrape
3 a rumpus
verb
to make off

shibboleth
noun
1 the criterion, catchword or catchphrase of a group, party or sect by which members may be identified
2 a slogan
3 a peculiarity of speech
&➤According to Judges chapter 12 verse 6, the Gileadites would ask a stranger to say the word 'shibboleth', the Hebrew word for an ear of corn or a stream, in order to check if he were in fact an Ephraimaite, and therefore an enemy. The Ephraimites could not pronounce the sound 'sh' and therefore could be easily identified by this test.

siffleur or siffleuse
noun
a male or female professional whistler

simony
noun
the buying or selling of an ecclesiastical benefice
&➤I would definitely pay the church a large sum before I die in the hope of spending a shorter time or no time at all in purgatory.

skutterudite
noun
a cubic mineral, cobalt arsenide

slacklining
noun
the sport of walking on a slack nylon rope tied between two points, for example over a chasm

slammakin or slammerkin
(obsolete)
noun
1 a loose gown
2 a slovenly-dressed woman, a slattern
adjective
slovenly

slapsauce
noun
a person who enjoys eating fine food

slickenside
noun
(geology) a smooth, polished or striated rock surface produced by friction

slip-string
noun
(dialect) a rogue, someone who richly deserves hanging

smad
verb
to cover with dirt

smell-feast
noun
(obsolete) a sponger
 &rwarr;This word creates a vivid image of someone so skilled at scrounging off others that they can actually smell a feast at some distance.

smerle
noun
a variety of domestic pigeon

snickersnee
(obsolete)
noun
1 a large knife for fighting
2 fighting with knives
verb
to fight with knives
 &rwarr;This is apparently from Dutch *steken* meaning 'to thrust' and *snijden* meaning 'to cut'.

snirt
noun
(Scots) a smothered laugh

snook, snoke or snowk
verb
1 to sniff or smell about
2 to lurk, prowl or sneak about

snootful
noun
enough alcohol to make one drunk
This is an unusual measurement in that it is totally unmeasurable.

snoozle
verb
to nuzzle and then sleep

snuzzle
verb
1 to grub or root
2 to rub or poke and sniff
3 to nuzzle

solecism
noun
1 a breach of syntax or a nonstandard grammatical usage
2 any absurdity, impropriety, or incongruity
3 a breach of good manners or etiquette

solifluxion or solifluction
noun
(geology) the slow movement of soil or scree down a slope resulting from alternate freezing and thawing

solipsism

noun

(philosophy) the theory that holds that self-existence is the only certainty, otherwise described as absolute egoism

somnambulism

noun

1 walking in sleep

2 a hypnotic trance in which acts are performed that are not remembered afterwards

sonopuncture

noun

a form of treatment that uses ultrasound to stimulate acupuncture points

sonsy or sonsie

adjective

(Scots)

1 bringing luck

2 comely

3 comfortable-looking

4 good-natured

5 plump, buxom

6 robust

> ❧This versatile Scots word is derived from Gaelic *sonas* meaning 'good fortune'. The Burns poem 'Address to a Haggis' begins with the words:
>> Fair fa' yer honest sonsie face,
>> Great chieftain o the puddin'-race!

soogee or soogie

noun

(nautical) a solution of soap, soda, etc for cleaning the decks and paintwork of a ship

sook

noun

1 (Australian) a soft, timid or cowardly person

2 (dialect) someone who sucks up fawningly, a toady

Soroptimist
adjective
of an international organization of clubs for professional women
noun
a member of one of these clubs
꙰This is a blend of Latin *soror* meaning 'sister', and 'optimist'.

sottisier
noun
a collection of jokes, ridiculous remarks, quotes, etc

spadix
noun
a fleshy spike of flowers

spang
(dialect)
noun
1 a bound; a leap
2 a sudden movement or blow
3 a bang
verb
1 to bound, spring
2 to dash
3 to fling
4 to throw or cause to spring into the air
adverb
(US) bang, exactly, straight, absolutely

spang-cockle
noun
(dialect) the flicking of a marble, etc from the forefinger with the thumbnail

spanghew
verb
to fling into the air, especially in a see-saw game using a plank,
originally from a practice of torturing frogs using a stick

⇛The *English Dialect Dictionary* of 1904 sheds a fascinating light on
the origin and meanings of this strange word. The mysterious frog
torturing practice seems to have been popular throughout Great
Britain, and is explained in graphic detail: 'Spanghewing was a cruel
custom amongst lads of blowing up a frog by inserting a straw under
the skin at the anus; the inflated frog was then jerked into the middle
of the pond by being put on a cross stick, the other end being struck, so
that the frog jumped high in the air'. Frogs were not the only victims of
this game; birds and other small animals were also flung to their deaths
in the same bizarre way.

spatterdash
noun
1 (US) roughcast
2 an old type of long gaiter or legging to protect the trouser leg from
being spattered with mud, etc

spelunker
noun
a person who explores caves as a hobby

speos
noun
a grotto-temple or tomb

sphairistike
noun
the name under which lawn tennis was patented in 1874 by Walter
Wingfield, and by which it was quite widely known for a time

⇛This is from Greek *sphairistike techne* meaning 'the art of playing
ball', from *sphaira* meaning 'a ball'. The pronunciation of this word is
'sfee-*ris*-tik-i', with the stress on the second syllable. One imagines that
the pronunciation contributed towards its surrender to the rather less
demanding 'tennis'.

spikenard
noun
1 an Indian herb
2 an aromatic oil or balsam from this herb
3 a synthetic substitute for this oil

spilth
noun
1 anything spilt or poured out lavishly
2 excess

spindrift
noun
1 the spray blown from the crests of waves
2 fine snow or sand driven by wind

spintry
noun
a male prostitute

spizzerinctum
noun
1 impudence or nerve
2 determination or zeal

spoffish or spoffy
adjective
(archaic) fussy, officious

spoffskins
noun
a prostitute pretending to be a man's wife

spuddle
verb
to dig superficially

squabash
verb
to crush, smash, defeat
noun
a crushing blow

squintifego
adjective
(obsolete) squinting

stalko
noun
(Anglo-Irish) a gentleman without fortune or occupation

stasivalence
noun
the condition of being able to have sexual intercourse only while standing

steampunk
noun
a literary genre that incorporates science fiction into a historical setting, often 19th-century England

steatopygous
adjective
fat-buttocked

stentorian
adjective
(of a voice) loud, powerful, carrying
&ന Stentor is a loud-voiced Greek herald in Homer's *Iliad*.

stercoricolous
adjective
living in dung

stereognosis
noun
the ability to establish the form and weight of an object by touch alone

stevedore
noun
a person who loads and unloads shipping vessels

stigmatophilia
noun
excessive enthusiasm for tattooing or body piercing

stigonomancy
noun
divination by writing on tree bark

stonesuck
noun
(obsolete) parsley

stooze
verb
to borrow money at zero or very low interest and invest it to make a profit

stotious or stocious
adjective
(Scots and Irish) drunk

stramash
(Scots)
noun
1 a tumult, a confused disturbance
2 a noisy argument
3 a wreck
verb
to wreck, smash

ငွ•One is likely to hear this word in football commentary, where an untidy attack on goal, met with some equally untidy defending, and involving quite a number of players, is often described as 'a goalmouth stramash'.

strumple
noun
the fleshy part of a horse's rear to which the tail is attached

suaveolent
adjective
fragrant
ငွ•This is pronounced 'swuh-*vee*-uh-luhnt', with the stress on the second syllable.

subaudition
noun
a sense understood or implied without being expressed

subumbrella
noun
the undersurface of a jellyfish's umbrella

sumpsimus
noun
a correct expression used in place of one that is popularly used but is strictly incorrect
ငွ•An example of a sumpsimus would be Hamlet's famous address to the skull, 'Alas, poor Yorick! I knew him, Horatio' in place of the incorrect, but oft-quoted 'Alas, poor Yorick! I knew him well'. See the entry for 'mumpsimus' for the etymology of 'sumpsimus'.

sundog
noun
a mock sun or parhelion

surcoat
noun
1 a medieval outer garment, usually sleeveless, often with heraldic devices, worn by men and women over armour or ordinary dress
2 an undershirt or waistcoat

swadge
verb
(Orkney) to sit and relax after eating

swordick
noun
a small eel-like coastal fish, the gunnel

Sybaritic
adjective
devoted to luxury

> The inhabitants of the Greek city of Sybaris in ancient Italy, the Sybarites, were renowned for their love of luxury.

Tt

tacamahac
noun
1 a gum-resin yielded by several tropical trees
2 the balsam poplar, or its resin

tachyphasia or tachyphrasia
noun
abnormally rapid or voluble speech

taghairm
noun
(Scots) (in the Scottish highlands) divination, especially inspiration sought by lying in a bullock's hide behind a waterfall

tapster
noun
a person who draws alcoholic drinks, a barperson
 This Old English-derived word which originally denoted a woman serving ale is probably less common now than the Italian *barista*.

tarabooka
noun
a drum-like instrument

taradiddle

noun
1 a fib, a lie
2 nonsense

tarantism

noun
(medical history) an epidemic dancing mania especially prevalent in southern Italy from the 15th to the 17th century, popularly thought to be caused by the tarantula bite

> ॐThe actual cause of this ailment remains unknown. It has been suggested that it was a kind of mass hysteria, or even a ruse to allow the sufferer to dance at the time when dancing was forbidden by religious order.

tathagatagarbha

noun
(Buddhism) the potential that is within each sentient being to become a Buddha

tatou

noun
an armadillo, especially the giant armadillo

tatterdemalion

noun
a tattered person, a ragamuffin
adjective
ragged, tattered, scarecrowlike

tattie-bogle

noun
(Scots) a scarecrow

tawdry

adjective
showy without taste or worth; gaudily adorned

noun
showy and worthless adornment
> ❧The origin of this word is an interesting one. It's a shortening of
> 'tawdry lace' which was a woman's silk necktie such as those sold at
> St Audrey's Fair, an annual fair at Ely. Audrey, whose proper name
> was Æthelthryth, was the daughter of the king of East Anglia. She
> developed a tumour in her throat and believed that it was God's
> punishment for her vanity because she had worn jewelled necklaces.
> Therefore, a gawdy necktie became known as 'St Audrey's lace' and
> thence 'tawdry lace'.

tchotchke
noun
1 an attractive trinket of no value
2 a pretty girl

temnospondylous
adjective
with vertebrae that have some elements separate

terpsichorean
adjective
of or relating to dancing
> ❧In Greek mythology Terpsicore was the muse of dancing.

teuchter
noun
(Scots)
1 a term originally used by Lowland Scots for a Highlander, especially
a Gaelic-speaker
2 any unsophisticated country person

thanatophobia
noun
a morbid dread of death

thelytoky

noun

parthenogenetic production of female offspring only

☙The opposite of this, the production of males only, is 'arrhenotoky'.

thible or thivel

noun

a porridge-stick

thrawn

adjective

(Scots)

1 twisted, distorted

2 wry, deliberately perverse

☙The first, literal sense of this word, meaning 'physically twisted', was extended to the figurative sense meaning 'psychologically twisted', that is 'deliberately perverse'. This is by far the commonest sense of this word nowadays.

thropple

noun

1 the throat

2 the windpipe, especially of an animal

☙It is possible that this comes from Old English *throtbolla* meaning 'windpipe' or 'gullet'.

thrymsa

noun

an Anglo-Saxon gold coin, or its value

Thule

noun

1 an island six days north of Orkney discovered by Pytheas in the 4th century BC, variously identified as Shetland, Iceland, Norway and Jutland

2 the extreme limit, northernmost land (often called **ultima Thule**)

☙This is pronounced '*thyoo*-lee', with the stress on the first syllable.

thunder-plump
noun
a heavy fall of rain in a thunderstorm

thurifer
noun
a person who carries the thurible (a censer of burning incense) during a religious ceremony

tickety-boo
adjective
fine, satisfactory

tickly-benders
plural noun
1 thin ice that bends underfoot
2 a game played on such ice
&> 'Tickly-benders' is not a winter sport that has yet made an appearance in the Winter Olympics, which seems a shame. There would be some kudos attached to being recognized as the world's finest tickly-bender.

tintinnabulation
noun
bell-ringing

titter-totter or titter-me-torter
noun
(dialect) a see-saw

tittle
noun
1 a dot, stroke, accent, vowel point, contraction or punctuation mark
2 the smallest part

tittup
verb
to prance, skip about gaily
noun
a light springy step, a canter

titty-totty
adjective
(Norfolk) small

tmesis
noun
(rhetoric) the separation or splitting up of a word into parts by one or more intervening words
    🙠An example of tmesis is 'abso-bloody-lutely'.

tohu bohu
noun
chaos
    🙠This is an adaptation of Hebrew *thohu wa-bhohu* meaning 'emptiness and desolation' from Genesis chapter 1 verse 2.

tomomania
noun
a compulsion to perform surgery

Torschlusspanik
noun
a sense of anxiety often experienced by those approaching middle age, characterized by a fear that life is passing too quickly and one's opportunities are narrowing
    🙠This German word literally means 'gate' (*Tor*), 'shut' (*schluss*), 'panic' (*Panik*). Although it appears to be the very epitome of a late 20th-century, early 21st-century neurosis, it does in fact have a more serious and sinister origin. It first appeared in 1961 when the border between East and West Berlin was closed, before the start of the building of the Berlin Wall. People in the East suffered from Torschlusspanik – panic that the gates between East and West were closing literally, and there would be no way out. This panic proved to be justified.

tortulous
adjective
with swellings at regular intervals

torulin
noun
a vitamin in yeast

tosticated
adjective
(dialect) befuddled; perplexed

toxophily
noun
1 a love of archery
2 archery

tragus
noun
1 a small fleshy prominence at the entrance of the external ear
2 any of the hairs growing in the outer ear, especially from this part

tribble
noun
a horizontal frame with wires stretched across it for drying paper

trichotillomania
noun
a neurosis in which a person pulls out tufts of his or her own hair

trilith
noun
a form of megalithic monument consisting of two upright stones
supporting another lying crosswise

tringle
noun
a curtain rod

troland
noun
a unit of visual stimulation in optometry

>L T Troland was an American physicist.

trot-cozy
noun
a riding hood

trumpery
noun
showy and worthless stuff; rubbish; ritual foolery
adjective
showy but worthless

tuftaffety
(archaic)
noun
a taffeta with tufted pile
adjective
1 of or wearing tuftaffety
2 richly dressed

turbary
noun
1 the right to take peat from another's ground
2 a place where peat is dug

turdion or tordion
noun
a dance similar to, but less spirited than, a galliard, especially common in the 15th and 16th centuries

turnspit
noun
1 a person who turns a spit
2 a long-bodied, short-legged dog employed to drive a wheel by which roasting-spits were turned

>This breed of dog, the turnspit dog, is now extinct. The physical demands of turning a roasting spit meant that they were often worked in shifts. When you are next in Abergavenny, visit the museum and see the stuffed turnspit dog, Whiskey, on display.

tussie mussie
noun
a small bunch of flowers, a posy

tutty
noun
crude zinc oxide

twitten or twitting
noun
a narrow lane between two walls or hedges

Uu

uberous
adjective
1 yielding an abundance of milk
2 abounding

uglyography
noun
poor handwriting

ulotrichous
adjective
woolly-haired

umami
noun
a savoury, satisfying taste, like that of monosodium glutamate
adjective
having such a taste
    ›This word is Japanese, and translates as 'savoury flavour.' It has been proposed that umami should be added to the currently accepted four basic tastes – sweet, salt, sour and bitter.

umbilicoplasty
noun
plastic surgery to improve the appearance of the navel

unau
noun
the two-toed sloth

uncautelous
adjective
incautious

undine
noun
according to Paracelsus, a water spirit that can obtain a human soul by bearing a child to a human husband

unguligrade
adjective
walking on hoofs

unstercorated
adjective
not having had manure applied

unwhig
verb
to cause (a person) to give up his or her Whig beliefs

up-Helly-Aa
noun
a midwinter festival, representing an older Celtic fire festival, held on the last Tuesday of January in Lerwick, Shetland, and now including guisers (people dressed up in costume) and the ceremonial burning of a Viking ship
> ৼ▸This comes from *up* meaning 'at the end, finished' and Scots *haliday* meaning 'holiday'.

urediniospore
noun
(botany) a spore produced by rust-fungi in its summer stage

usufruct

noun

the right to use and profit from another's property on the condition
that it remains uninjured; life-rent

verb

to hold in usufruct

> ☙This term from Roman law also exists in Scots law. Unsurprisingly
> it is a Latin word, from *usus* meaning 'use' and *fructus* meaning
> 'enjoyment'.

Vv

vade-mecum

noun

a useful handbook that one carries about with one for constant reference, a pocket companion

    ❧This constant companion is following the Latin instruction *vade* meaning 'go' and *mecum* meaning 'with me'.

valetudinarian

noun

a person who is constantly anxious and fanciful about the state of his or her health

    ❧The father of the eponymous *Emma* in Jane Austen's novel is described as follows: 'for having been a valetudinarian all his life, without activity of mind or body, he was a much older man in ways than in years'.

vasovagal

adjective

relating to the effect of the vagus nerve on blood pressure and circulation

vaticide

noun

the killer or killing of a prophet

velocipede
noun
1 an early form of bicycle, originally one propelled by the feet on the ground
2 (obsolete) a swift-footed person
adjective
swift of foot
verb
to ride a velocipede
> ⪧The image of someone riding a velocipede brings to mind the cartoon character Fred Flintstone driving his Stone-Age car.

velology
noun
the collecting of expired car tax discs as a hobby
> ⪧Another curious hobby of the British male, but it appears to be a comparatively new one and has been commented on by the press.

ventripotent
adjective
(facetious) with great capacity or appetite for food

verbigerate
verb
to repeat certain words or phrases at short intervals in a purposeless manner, as occurs in schizophrenia

verruciform
adjective
wartlike

verticordious
adjective
able to turn the heart from evil to good

vespertine
adjective
1 of or relating to the evening
2 happening, opening, appearing, active, or setting, in the evening

vesuvium
noun
(archaic) a slow-burning match for lighting a cigarette or pipe

vibraslap
noun
a percussion instrument consisting of a bent wire with a wooden ball at one end, and a wooden block with metal teeth at the other
> ໑⸱Also called the mandible, this percussion instrument makes a sound akin to teeth rattling. It is said to be the modern descendent of primitive musical instruments which used the jawbones of donkeys or zebras.

viduous
adjective
1 widowed
2 empty

viliaco, villiaco, viliago or villiago
noun
(obsolete) a coward

viliority
noun
(rare) the quality of being worthless or vile

vincristine
noun
an alkaloid substance derived from the Madagascar or rosy periwinkle (*Catharanthus roseus*), used in a treatment of certain types of leukaemia

viscacha
noun
a South American burrowing rodent of heavy build

vitrain
noun
a separable constituent of bright coal, of vitreous appearance

Vitruvian
adjective
1 of or in the style of Vitruvius Pollio, a Roman architect under the emperor Augustus
2 denoting a kind of convoluted scrollwork
   ⹀Marcus Vitruvius Pollio was a Roman architect, engineer and writer of the 1st century BC. The adjective 'Vitruvian' is mostly familiar today through the famous Vitruvian Man drawing by Leonardo da Vinci. This shows a nude man drawn in two positions (with legs together and with legs slightly apart) within a circle and a square. Leonardo based the drawing on Vitruvius's notes on the geometrical proportions of the ideal human body.

vittate
adjective
1 (botany) (of some fruits) having a thin, elongated cavity containing oil within its pericarps
2 (zoology) striped lengthwise

vivisepulture
noun
(rare) burial alive

Vodun
noun
a West African religion that worships a large range of deities, including the spirits of trees, rivers, rocks, etc

vug

noun

(Cornish) a cavity in a rock, usually lined with crystals

 ❧This was the name given by Cornish miners to such cavities and it comes from the Cornish word *vooga*.

vuvuzela

noun

a plastic instrument that, when blown, makes a noise similar to the trumpeting of an elephant

 ❧This word may seem strange now but one suspects it will be rather more familiar when the football World Cup kicks off in South Africa, the home of the vuvuzela, in June 2010.

Ww

wabbit
adjective
(Scots) exhausted, tired out

waftage
noun
transportation through air or across water

wag-at-the-wa'
noun
(Scots and Northern English) a hanging clock with exposed pendulum and weights

wagyu
noun
one of four breeds of Japanese beef cattle that produce highly prized meat
> The wagyu cattle produce the meat known as kobe beef. These cattle have a diet that includes saki and beer, and they have daily massage that helps ensure maximum tenderness in the beef.

walla-walla
noun
a type of motorboat used as a taxi in Victoria Harbour, Hong Kong

ह‍The motorboat was nicknamed 'walla-walla' by European visitors in imitation of the noise made by its engine.

wallsend

noun

1 originally, coal dug at Wallsend on Tyneside
2 later, coal of a certain quality and size

ह‍The town of Wallsend takes its name from the fact that it is located at the end of Hadrian's Wall.

wallydrag or wallydraigle

noun

(Scots)

1 a person or animal that is feeble, worthless or slovenly
2 the youngest of a family

Walpurgis night

noun

the eve of the first of May, when witches, according to German popular superstition, rode on broomsticks and male goats to revel with their master the devil, especially on the Brocken in the Harz Mountains

ह‍May 1 is the feast day of Saint Walpurga, an English missionary who became abbess of the convent at Heidenheim and who was canonized around 870 AD.

wanchancy or wanchancie

adjective

(Scots) unlucky, dangerous or uncanny

wanderoo

noun

1 a name usually applied to the lion-tailed macaque, a native of the Malabar coast of India
2 properly, a langur of Sri Lanka

wang
noun
(obsolete)
1 the cheek
2 a molar tooth
　§►This comes from an Old English word *wange*.

wankle
adjective
(dialect)
1 unstable, unsteady; changeable
2 not to be depended upon

wanthriven
adjective
(Scots) stunted; ill-grown; emaciated

wanty
noun
1 (obsolete) a belt used to secure a load on a pack-horse's back
2 (dialect) the belly-band of a shaft-horse
3 (dialect) a short rope, especially one used for binding hay on a cart

wapper-eyed
adjective
blinking

wappet
noun
a yelping cur

warth
noun
(dialect) a ford

waveson
noun
(rare) goods floating on the sea after a shipwreck

wayzgoose or wasegoose
noun
formerly, a printers' annual dinner or picnic

wazzock
noun
(informal) a stupid or foolish person

weanling
noun
a child or animal newly weaned
> ᕦ➤This comes from Old English *wenian* meaning 'to accustom'. It is not related to the Scots word for a child 'wean' which is a contraction of 'wee ane' which means 'little one'.

weather gleam
noun
(dialect) a bright aspect of the sky at the horizon

weequashing
noun
the spearing of eels or fish from a canoe at night by torchlight
> ᕦ➤This odd-sounding word is from Algonquian *wigwas* meaning 'bark of the birch tree' (and hence a canoe made of birch bark).

weirdiana
plural noun
weird or bizarre things as collectibles

Welsummer
noun
a breed of large poultry with golden plumage, prolific egg-layers
> ᕦ➤This chicken was first bred in the Dutch village of Welsum.

whangam
noun
an imaginary animal
> ᕦ➤Oliver Goldsmith coined this word in his work *Citizen of the World*:

'so the whangam eat the grasshopper, the serpent in the whangam, the yellow bird the serpent, and the hawk the yellow bird'.

Wharncliffe order
noun
a standing order in Parliament that requires that, if the directors of a company wish to promote a private bill to extend that company's powers, they must first secure the agreement of the shareholders (at a **Wharncliffe meeting**)

wheatear
noun
any of various songbirds with a white rump
> ৡ◈You might be wondering why the bird is called 'wheatear' when it's got a white bottom. Well, it's likely that 'wheatear' is a corruption of 'white arse'.

whiffler
noun
(history) an official who clears the way for a procession
> ৡ◈It is possible that this comes from an obsolete word *wifel* meaning 'javelin' or 'battle-axe'. Although this is a historical word, one is reminded of the scenes that attended the procession of the Olympic torch through various cities in Spring 2008, and the Chinese bodyguards who formed a protective ring around the torch on its route.

whigmaleerie
noun
(Scots)
1 a trinket or knick-knack
2 a fantastic ornamentation
3 a whim

whippletree
noun
the crosspiece of a carriage, plough, etc, which is made so as to swing on a pivot and to which the traces of a harnessed animal are fixed

whippoorwill

noun

a species of nightjar native to North America

> ᧞The name is imitative of the bird's call. The whippoorwill makes an appearance in one of country music's best-loved songs, Hank Williams' 'I'm so lonesome I could cry.'

whittie-whattie

(Scots)

verb

1 to mutter, to whisper

2 to shilly-shally

noun

1 vague language intended to deceive

2 a frivolous excuse

wibble

verb

1 to speak foolishly

2 to talk at length about inconsequential matters

widdy

noun

(dialect)

1 a rope, especially one made of willow twigs

2 a halter for hanging

williewaught

noun

(Scots) a deep draught of alcohol

> ᧞This is in fact a misunderstanding of a phrase in what must be Robert Burns' best-known poem, 'Auld Lang Syne'. In the last verse the line is 'And we'll tak a right guid-willie-waught'. 'Guid-willie' means 'goodwill', so the phrase actually means 'a generous and friendly draught' rather than a deep one. But the 'deep draught' misunderstanding is the one that has stuck.

williwaw
noun
1 a gust of cold wind blowing seawards from a mountainous coast, eg in the Straits of Magellan
2 a sudden squall
3 a tumult or disturbance

wimble
noun
an instrument for boring holes, turned by a handle

winx
verb
(obsolete) to bray like a donkey

withershins or widdershins
adverb
(Scots) in the contrary direction, contrary to the course of the sun
ॐThis is the opposite of 'deasil'.

wittol
noun
(archaic) a man who knows his wife's unfaithfulness, and accepts it

woodshedding
noun
spontaneous barber-shop singing
ॐIf the thought of this does not scare you, then you are without fear.

woodwose or woodhouse
noun
1 a wild man of the woods
2 a satyr, faun

worricow, worrycow or wirricow
noun
(Scots)
1 a hobgoblin

2 the devil
3 anything frightful or grotesque

woubit, woobut, oubit or oobit
noun
1 a hairy caterpillar, especially one of a tiger moth
2 a small and shabby person

wowf
adjective
(Scots) crazy

Xantippe or Xanthippe
noun
a scolding or bad-tempered woman
   📖Xanthippe was the wife of the philosopher Socrates.

xassafrassed
adjective
(US slang) pregnant

xenization
noun
the act of travelling as a stranger

xenodochium
noun
a building for the reception of strangers, especially a guest-house in a monastery

xerophagy
noun
the eating of dry food, or of bread, vegetables and water, as a form of fast

xyster
noun
a surgeon's instrument for scraping bones

Yy

yahoo
noun
a brutal or boorish lout
> ৼThis term derives from a race of brutish creatures, resembling men but with the understanding and passions of brutes, from Jonathan Swift's in Gulliver's Travels.

yakow
noun
an animal crossbred from a male yak and a domestic cow

yale
noun
a mythical animal, depicted in heraldry as resembling a horse with tusks, horns and an elephant's tail
> ৼThis comes from Latin *eale* which was an unidentified Ethiopian animal mentioned by the writer Pliny.

yegg
noun
(US) a burglar, especially a burglar of safes

Yeibichai
noun
a Navajo ceremony for curing serious illness, in which various gods are summoned and represented by masked dancers

Yerkish

noun

a language developed for use primarily by chimpanzees, involving
symbols that represent objects or ideas

> ☙This was developed by the German philosopher and psychologist
> Ernst von Glaserfeld for use in primate research at the Yerkes Regional
> Primate Research Centre in Atlanta, Georgia.

yikker

verb

(of an animal) to utter sharp little cries

noun

a cry like this

ylem

noun

the original substance from which, according to some theories, the
elements developed

> ☙This is pronounced '*ee*-luhm', with the stress on the first syllable.

yoof

(informal)

noun

youth, young people

adjective

(especially of magazines, TV or radio programmes, etc) relating to,
specifically aimed at, pandering to, or dealing with topics (thought to
be) of interest to modern youth

> ☙This word is based on the pronunciation of 'youth' in certain London
> accents. It is almost always used in a derogatory way.

yuke

verb

(dialect) to itch

noun

itching, the itch

> ☙This expressive word has many variant spellings, all equally suggestive

of an irritating tickle. These include youk, yeuk, yuck, euk and ewk. Related adjectives are yuky and yucky.

yump
verb
(in rally-driving) to leave the ground (in one's vehicle) when going over a ridge or crest
noun
an instance of this

&ent;The Norwegian word *jump* meaning 'jump' is pronounced 'yump'.

Zz

zalambdodont
adjective
having molar teeth with V-shaped ridges, as some Insectivora do

zarf or zurf
noun
an ornamental holder for a hot coffee cup

zelatrix, zelatrice or zelator
noun
a nun whose duty is to keep watch on the behaviour of the younger nuns in the convent, or on that of the mother superior

zetetic
adjective
proceeding by inquiry
noun
1 a search or investigation
2 a seeker

ziggurat
noun
a temple-tower in ancient Mesopotamia, much like a pyramid in shape, consisting of a number of storeys each successive one of which was smaller than the one below it

ziraleet
noun
a shout of joy among Arab women
> ⃕Those who have been guests in Berber houses of the Atlas or in the Sahara will be reminded of the extraordinary but pleasant sound of the ululation of the women. This 'music' contributes to the festivities of the menfolk from the hidden recesses of the roof cavity above.

zonesthesia
noun
a feeling as if the body is being constricted by a tight cord

zonk
(informal)
noun
1 a sharp blow
2 the sound of a swift, sharp or firm impact
verb
1 to hit sharply, or with a zonk
2 to blast
adverb
with a zonk

zoochlorella
noun
any of various green algae that live in the cytoplasm of many marine and freshwater invertebrates

zoozoo
noun
the wood pigeon
> ⃕This name is imitative of the sound made by the bird. There are many such birds: *kittiwake, twite, yaffle, bobolink, potoo, towhee, peewit, chewink, veery, chiffchaff, peewee, chough* and *killdeer* being just a few.

zufolo *or* zuffolo
noun
a small flute or flageolet used in training songbirds

zugzwang

noun

(chess) a blockade position in which any move is disadvantageous to the blockaded player

zumbooruk

noun

a small cannon mounted on a swivel, carried on the back of a camel

zwitterion

noun

(chemistry) an ion carrying both a positive and a negative charge

zythepsary

noun

(obsolete)

a brewery

zythum

noun

a kind of beer made by the ancient Egyptians, highly commended by Diodorus Siculus, a writer of the 1st century BC

Also available

'A treasure trove'
Susie Dent

ISBN: 978 0550 10329 1
Price: £9.99